The 1864 Diary of Mrs. Sarah Jane Rousseau

May 13, 1864 to Dec. 18, 1864

Pella, Iowa to San Bernardino, California

Edited by Janelle Molony

Copyright © 2023 by Janelle Molony

All rights reserved. No part of this book may be reproduced or used in any manner without written permission of the copyright owner except for the use of quotations in a book review or as permitted under fair use laws.

 M Press Publishing

Cover Design and Interior: J. Molony
Cover Image: Sarah Jane Daglish Rousseau, circa 1840. Attributed to American inventor and artist Samuel F.B. Morse. Courtesy of Richard Molony (Molony family collection).
Official Author Website: www.JanelleMolony.com

AISN: 979-8-394730702 (large print)
ISBN: 978-1-7344638-9-7 (large print)
Library of Congress: 203909248
Non-Fiction: U.S. History
Genres: Americana, Personal Diaries
Keywords: Iowa, Nebraska, Wyoming, Utah, Nevada, Arizona, California, Civil War, Sioux War, Wagon Train, Westward Migration, Oregon Trail, Overland-California Trail, Mormon Trail, Santa-Fe Trail, Family History, Research

Reader Reviews

"Perhaps the most dramatic pioneer exploits of all... belong to Sarah Jane Rousseau." **Tombstone Epitaph** (2019)

"A modern reader is struck with the delicacy [Sarah] Jane uses in her descriptions." **Pamela Greenwood,** Descendant of the Curtis family (2006)

"Of the hundreds of diaries written by pioneers traveling west ... the Rousseau Diary ... is among the most eloquent." **Nicholas R. Cataldo**, for the *Overland Journal* (2015)

"The Rousseau Diary will be especially interesting to all teachers and students of the Westward Movement." **Gerald Smith,** San Bernardino Co. Museum (2011)

Other Books in The Rousseau Series

From Where I Sat (Forthcoming). Fictionalized retelling of the Pella Company's 1864 Trip Across the Plains.

The Complete Annotated 1864 Diary of Sarah Jane Rousseau (Forthcoming). Sarah J. Rousseau's diary, supported with in-depth research notes, photographs, illustrations, maps, mileage and complete wagon train manifest and roster of all mentioned.

Emigrant Tales of the Platte River Raids (2023). Thrilling trail diary companion book featuring first-hand accounts and extensive research from the attacks of July 1864 in the "Black Hills of Idaho."

Dedicated to

Mrs. Sarah Jane Rousseau

You deserve to have your voice and your truth known and valued without having someone else filter or interpret it. Finally.

Table of Contents

Foreword	1
The 1864 Diary of Mrs. Sarah Rousseau	7
For Further Reading	313
Acknowledgements	319
A Sneak Peak...	321
About the Author & Editor	347

The 1864 Diary of Mrs. Sarah Jane Rousseau

Foreword

Sarah Jane Daglish Rousseau's diary may have once been a very small contribution to the journey her family took in the midst of the Civil War. Over time, it has been found to be a remarkable record of events and people who have become legends of the Wild West and those who have left incredible legacies as pioneers in their own respect. It is now not only a private family treasure, but also an item of serious importance to United States history.

The original item is currently in the Molony family estate. It is a small, leather-bound pocket-size book with lightly penciled-in sketches of nightly camp corrals. Pressed between the delicate pages are dried wildflowers that Sarah collected along the way. The elegant cursive and vocabulary reflect Sarah's upbringing as a member of the Landed Gentry near London, England.

The 1864 Diary of Mrs. Sarah Jane Rousseau

Sarah was born in 1815, at the height of the Industrial Revolution. She and her older sister were raised with fineries, well-educated and highly talented in music and needlework. The Daglish family emigrated to the United States in the early 1830s, then both girls attended finishing school at the Abbott Institute outside of New York City. From there, the Daglishes moved to Michigan, where both girls are suspected to have taught piano at the Detroit Female Seminary boarding school in Kalamazoo. There, Sarah met her future husband, James Rousseau. He was a medical student from Kentucky, visiting the area with his cousin and future Major General on the 1864 Vice-Presidential election ticket, Lovell Harrison Rousseau.

After spending some time in Kentucky on the Rousseau Plantation (also known as the "Montgomery Mansion"), Dr. James and Sarah Rousseau traveled by ferry to the unincorporated forest of Elm Grove, in what would become Liberty Township in Marion County, Iowa. Sarah continued teaching piano but her rheumatoid arthritis soon saw her fully wheelchair bound. Her husband, a well-known local physician, had no better answer than to pack up the family and make the journey to a warmer, drier climate.

Fortunately, another Marion County resident, Provost Marshal Nicholas Earp, and one of James Rousseau's closest friends, Israel Curtis, were ready to make that journey as well. Together, with the family of John Hamilton, the four traveling parties left their politically charged state in favor of freedom and fresh soil.

The editor cautions readers who have sought for or used alternative and partial versions that have been produced by others. Each version is problematic for different reasons. In the early 2000's, a newspaper from Iowa produced *Day By Day Diary*, a serialized version for public consumption that altered Sarah's

The 1864 Diary of Mrs. Sarah Jane Rousseau

original writing. In 2002, Earl Chafin self-published a version titled, *The Rousseau Diary,* with significant fallacies in his conclusions that are misleading to researchers and family historians. In 1958, a selection from the diary was published by the San Bernardino County Museum Association that only pertains to California history and incorrectly assigns authorship to Dr. James Rousseau. To eliminate further confusion, the Molony family has determined it best to release the full, unaltered text from Mrs. Sarah Jane Rousseau herself. The intent is to provide clarity and preserve historical integrity in future educational and research applications.

The following copy of Mrs. Sarah Jane Rousseau's diary is the only complete and authenticated version that has been scrupulously preserved by descendants of the Curtis and Rousseau families. In the 1950s, Hon. J. W. Curtis, Sr. created an initial transcription from the original document, then belonging to Walter

The 1864 Diary of Mrs. Sarah Jane Rousseau

Beverly Molony (my grandparent by marriage), to which I am ever grateful for as a head start on this project. As much as possible, Sarah's original spelling and grammar are intact, though paragraphing and punctuation additions have been incorporated to support reading clarity.

Enjoy the adventure!

Janelle Molony, Editor

3rd great-granddaughter of James and Sarah Rousseau

The 1864 Diary of Mrs. Sarah Jane Rousseau

The 1864 Diary of Mrs. Sarah Jane Rousseau

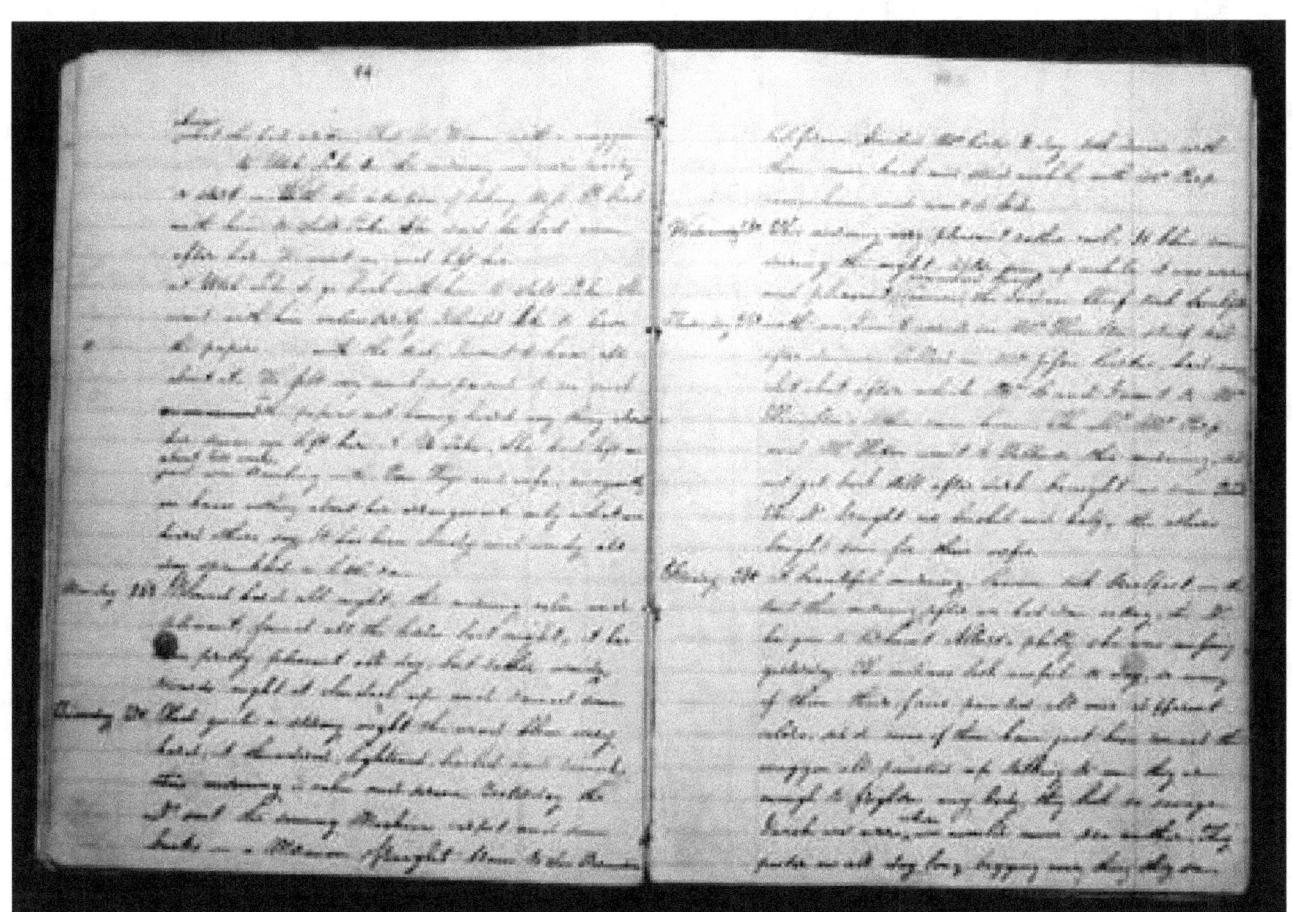

Photograph of the original Rousseau diary.
Courtesy of Nicolas Cataldo.

The 1864 Diary of
Mrs. Sarah Jane Rousseau

Start: May 13, 1864 from Liberty Township, Iowa

The 1864 Diary of Mrs. Sarah Jane Rousseau

Friday 13th [May]

The Pella Company reached Knoxville to-day about 2 o'clock[.]

It is quite pleasant and warm.

Saturday 14th [May]

Started from Knoxville on the 14th, after bidding all farewell. The weather is pleasant and warm.

Reached the camp ground about 4 o'clock. It is some 2 miles from Pleasantville, quite a pleasant place.

The 1864 Diary of Mrs. Sarah Jane Rousseau

We have just done eating supper. To look around it looks a great deal like living out of doors.

Sunday 15th [May]

Another beautiful morning. Just done eating breakfast.

Eat dinner and supper and then went to bed.

Monday 16th [May]

Got up and prepared breakfast. After eating[,] all confusion getting ready to start. I can't describe the appearance of all things as they really are. But the weather is indeed beautiful. All nature seems smiling. The birds singing their lively song of praise unto the Most High God.

We started and went through Sandyville, then as far as the lower River, about 10 miles from Pleasantville. So here we have camped for the night.

Just done eating supper and getting ready for bed. The girls talking of fishing some tonight. Elizabeth and Mattie have been riding horseback most of the day. John has been riding his mare most of the time and Albert most of his.

[**On the back of this first page the following statement is found:** "The Dr. sent the sewing machine, carpet and some books with a Mormon train going to California, San Bernardino. The Mormons name is Guard."][1]

Tuesday 17th [May]

The woods are alive with the sweet music of birds. Another delightful morning. The girls caught no fish last night. Seven more waggons made their appearance after we pitched our tent.

We will soon be ready to start again. The girls and boys have been laughing, fit to kill themselves, at a remark Tom made "That he must go to John B's after this thinking bob." Libby snorted right out, it was at the breakfast.

---

[1] This entry relates to September 26-27.

We did not get off this morning as I thought we should. We were detained on account of Jesse Curtis['] cow running off. I hope he will be here tonight.

Jesse has come. Could not find his cow and now one of our horses has run off. Tom has started after her.

He returned this morning bringing her along. He had to go the other side of Pleasantville about one mile before he got her. Some man saw her and put her in a stable.

Wednesday 18th [May]

Beautiful morning. The birds are singing delightfully. I suppose we will make this start after breakfast.

Got to Indianola about noon. The County seat of Warren. It is quite a nice little town. About the size of Knoxville. I think Warren a pretty Co. The prairies are very large and rolling. It makes Marion look rather in the shade. There are some very pretty farms around Indianola. The people seem to display some considerable taste.

We rolled on after shopping a little. And went about 8 miles. So here we are camped just at the edge of some timber.

Thursday 19th [May]

Another beautiful morning exceedingly warm. We are just ready for a start.

Got off about 7 o'clock. Stopped at a Creek and fed.

Passed through the little town of St. Charles. Traveled on and after 17 miles travel arrived at Middle River where we were detained again on account of Curtis losing a cow.

Friday 20th [May]

Started in the afternoon and passed through Winterset, the county seat of Madison[.] Camped 2 miles w. of that town.

Traveled this day 4 1/2 miles, came 2 or three miles s.w. of Winterset camped on the Prairie a very pleasant place.

Saturday 21st [May]

Still on the Prairie waiting for Mr. Curtis. It is a very pleasant morning[,] rather windy[,] blew hard all day[,] prospect of rain.

Mr. C. not come yet. We can sing with great propriety "Out on the Prairie."

Mr. Curtis has come. We have had quite a nice shower.

Sunday 22nd [May]

Cleared off about ready to start.
Stopped at noon and fed. Down on the Middle River.

Camp for the night. Still blowing hard.

Come 14 miles to-day.

Monday 23rd [May]

Started[.] Crossed Grand River Adair Co. Traveled on to a little town called Greenfield. The Prairies are very large and rolling.

We went on until we came to a quarter of a mile of Fantonelle, the county seat, which we left, taking the right hand rode.

Went a few miles farther and camped on the Prairie.

Tuesday 24th [May]

Cold and windy. I did not think there was so much barren country in Iowa for miles[.] So far as your eye can reach[,] not a tree or shrub to be seen, but a far wilderness of Prairie.

Went on and crossed a branch of the Nodowa. Went a mile farther and camped on the prairie.

Wednesday 25th [May]

A pretty morning[.] About ready to start[.]

Rode about 15 miles to Lewis, the County seat of Cass, quite a nice little town built close by the Nishinabotny River[,] a very pretty stream[.]

Went a few miles farther, got where we found good grass and water and camped for the night at Walnut Creek.

Thursday 26th [May]

A pleasant morning rather cool, determined on account of Mr. C., he had not come, got tired waiting and travelled about 10 miles, stopped to water and feed our horses.

Mr. C. not come yet, went on 10 miles and crossed West Nishinabotny River about 25 miles from Council Bluffs.

Friday 27th [May]

Another beautiful morning, the birds singing beautifully, we have been greatly blessed with splendid weather and safe traveling. I feel thankful to our Heavenly Father for his watchful and tender care over us.

Traveled on passed over Mud Creek, Mills County, from thence to Silver Creek Patawatimy Co., went within 3 miles of Council Bluffs and camp for the night on Musquite Creek.

Saturday 28th [May]

Pa went to the Bluffs to-day and stayed until about night. It has been very warm all day. Expected to get a letter from Mary Ann but was disappointed.

Sunday 29th [May]

Went onto Council Bluffs[.] It is quite a large city, but don't appear too much advantage on account of the Bluffs[.] Sometime you will see a very pretty building, built as it were on a ledge, and at one side and the back a high bluff apparently not more than a couple of yards from the house.

Pa went to the Occulist to have his eye operated on, the occulist said there was a scum growing over it, he thinks he can cure it. Got a letter from Mary Ann to-day.

We are now camped close by a Lake near the Missouri R.[,] very muddy looking water[.] There is plenty whitecaps to-day, the wind is very high and it is extremely warm.

We can see Omaha quite plain from where we are camped, it is about 4 miles distant looking through the Marine glass[.] It brings us pretty close by.

Monday 30th [May]

Pleasant morning[.] The girls are washing to-day, we want the ironing and all done up. We think of crossing the Missouri River to-morrow, to commence our long journey across the Plains.

Tuesday 31st [May]

Finished the ironing, done some baking, our company thought they would be ready to start by that time.

Wednesday June 1st

Had quite a pleasant shower this morning, cleared off, thought we would leave here to-day but detained on account of our company not being ready.

I had two ladies call to see me this morning, one of them knew me in Burlington[,] had been to our house several times. I did not know her[,] she was then quite a small girl but the Dr. knew her, her name is Hanton the other lady was Mrs. Babbitt.

We had quite a pleasant visit[.] They were full of their fun[.] They are strong Democrats[.] They talk of going to California next spring if they can sell out.

Thursday 2nd [June]

A very pleasant morning, still camped by the Lake waiting for our company. The Dr. has gone to see what is the matter that they are not here. He rode 10 or 15 miles[,] came back and said they had all crossed the River yesterday forenoon. So we packed up as soon as possible and started for the ferry, got there about one o'clock.

Dick Curtis was on the boat coming after us, he said one of his little brothers fell out of their waggon and was very badly hurt. He had to wait until the ferry boat went over and back again before we could cross there is so many going.

At last we got over to Nebraska[,] Omaha City, it is quite a large place, got a number of pretty buildings, a much more slightly place than Council Bluffs. We laughed to see them shake the dust of Iowa from off their feet, and getting [out] from under the dominion of Bill Stone.

The girls had their likeliness taken in their bloomer costume. We went to the P.O. thought we might get a letter from Mary Ann but was disappointed.

We had some rain this afternoon, it turned real cold. Went two miles and camped on the prairie, met our company, a very poor camping place neither wood or grass.

Friday 3rd [June]

Very cool and cloudy, soon be ready to start.

Traveled about 10 miles, it has cleared off pleasant and warm[.]

Stopped at noon to feed our horses[.] The prairies are very large, houses scattering, wind blowing so hard I can hardly write.

Went as far as Elk Horn[,] 22 miles from Omaha, Douglas Co. intend camping here[.] Have to guard at night now. Something frightened our horses and they broke loose which caused a good deal of confusion for a while.

Traveled 20 miles to-day.

Saturday 4th [June]

Crossed Elk Horn River about mile and half West of Elk Horn City[.] Very cool this morning[.]

Wind high[,] traveled 8 miles, stopped at noon to feed, traveled 9 miles farther[,] went about 2 miles West of Fremont[,] Dodge County. The wind has been dreadful high all day.

We had considerable of a thunderstorm and very nice shower this afternoon after which the wind abated some[.]

Made 17 miles to-day. We are in Douglas County this evening.

Sunday 5th [June]

A very pleasant morning, the birds are singing merrily, all looks bright and clear.

Went about 15 miles and stopped for noon at the North Bend of Platte River. Tried to form a corral for the first time, found we could not get grass for our horses and we went about a mile farther where we found enough grass for our horses and stopped for noon[.] The rest stayed where they were as they all had corn to feed with and we had fed all of ours out.

As we went[,] we saw some half naked Indians[.] They seemed as if they were shooting their bows and arrows[.]

About 3 o'clock in the afternoon[,] the rest of our company came along and we rode a few miles farther looking for good grass[.]

At last Mr. Earp spied some good grass close by a house[.] He thought he would ask permission for us to camp there but the woman would not let us go. She looked like a low Dutch or Irish woman[,] I don't know which[.] She gave them all Jessy, the boys would jaw back to her and made her so mad. Mr. Earp said she cussed him like everything.

Went about half a mile to the North Bend of the Platte River where we stopped for the night, a very pretty camping place, pleasant evening rather cool.

Went 22 miles to-day.

Monday 6th [June]

Very cool this morning, rather foggy.

Went about a mile and crossed Shell Creek, a very nice stream, watered our horses and went about 10 miles and stopped to noon[.] There is scarcely anything to relieve the eye, nothing but an immense Prairie or Plain which is indeed the most proper name, occasionally a little timber along the Creeks and River and sometimes pass by a farm house and every 15 or 20 miles past a Ranche. If I had to live here[,] I should think of living out of the world.

We have heard several times they feared trouble with the Indians but I hope there is nothing of it as we have not seen many yet. There was four among our camp this morning[.] They say they are Pawnese. There was one Indian come and stood by us a good while. I was writing some in my Journal. He wanted to know what I was studying, he said you are curious people. He wanted me to give him some matches and some soap. We did not give them anything and they took their leave[.] We are just getting among them, I am afraid they will be troublesome[.]

Went 15 miles to-day.

Tuesday 7th [June]

Looked some like rain this morning but it is now clearing off. I think we shall have a pleasant day[.]

We have traveled about 9 miles to a place called Columbus[,] the County seat of Platt Co. Quite a small town[.] Crossed Loup Fork[,] the North branch of the Platte River, a bad place to cross full of quick sand[.]

We went onto the ferry boat as far as we could to a small island, about two thirds of the way across the river, then we had to go the rest of the way as fast as possible for fear we should stick[.] It was considerable trouble to get all the waggons across. I was really glad when we got across safely.

Tonight the Dr. and three others have to watch[,] the Indians are pretty thick here and getting rather troublesome a good many coming around whenever we stop. The Dr. was up all night[,] feels about sick this morning. Went 17 miles.

We wrote a letter to Mary Ann and sent their likenesses, Elizabeth and Mattie, and mailed it at Columbus[,] the County seat of Platte County.

The 1864 Diary of Mrs. Sarah Jane Rousseau

Wednesday 8th [June]

Cloudy this morning[,] almost ready to start[.]

Did not make much of a ride to-day. Did not ride more than [fifteen] miles, found a good place for grass and water and camped for the night[.]

Went 15 miles to-day.

Thursday 9th [June]

A very pleasant morning[,] about ready to start.

Came about 10 miles and stopped for noon, it has been dreadfully warm to-day. I think the thermometer must have been pretty near a hundred[.]

It clouded up this afternoon and seemed to have every appearance of a storm, the wind raised pretty smartly for a while and made it much more pleasant for us to travel[.]

We passed this afternoon a lone grave, it appeared recently made. I suppose some poor emigrant on his way, perhaps to fortune[.] It seems sad to see such a sight on the Plains.

We have traveled about 23 miles to-day and have now come close by the River. It is some cloudy I think it will likely rain to-night[.] I hope it will lay the dust, it almost smothers us.

Friday 10th [June]

A pleasant morning. Missed John's mare[.] The Dr. went to hunt her[.] He has returned bringing the mare along.

We passed another grave this morning, it was a man that died last August. We passed the Lone Tree Ranche this morning, we are now about 130 miles from Omaha.

Went a few miles and camped for the night[.] It has turned quite cool and some appearance of rain[.]

Traveled 22 miles to-day.

Saturday 11th [June]

Rained a few sprinkles this morning[,] still cool and cloudy. I think it will rain.

Rode about 10 miles [to] Grand Island city, a very small place. The Telegraph office is here, went on a little farther and camped, intend doing some washing[.] The girls washed and I walked to Mrs. McCully's waggon with the help of a chair and taking hold of the waggon wheels and tongue as I passed along. I hope I will be able to walk soon[.]

We have travelled some 14 miles to-day, it is still very cold and dry.

Sunday 12th [June]

Some cloudy this morning and very cool and dry. I wish we had enough rain to lay the dust[.] Mrs. Hays[,] Mrs. Curtis's is daughter[,] is sick. The Dr. thinks she is taking the fever. Mr. Curtis's is little boy that fell out of the waggon and got so badly hurt is getting better. We intend camping here to-day.

It has been a very pleasant day although a very lonesome one to me, nothing to elevate or enliven the mind, when I look around me and see and know how our Sabbath is spent, I long for the time to come when I can keep that Holy Day in a more acceptable manner.

This part of the country is more thickly settled than farther back, the farms are tolerable, the houses[,] most of them rather curious[.] They are very low buildings and some few of the roofs are singled, but most of them are covered with dirt and some of them are pretended to be thatched[.] We have passed a good many houses they call Adobe that is made of dirt[.] A good many of the farms are without any fences when other are fenced only one side, that next to the road.

The road runs close by the Telegraph poles[,] the timber mostly cottonwood[.] Bought some Buffalo meat to-day, it is very nice and tender.

Monday 13th [June]

A very cool morning and cloudy, pretty near ready to rain[.]

Another start, rode about 6 miles and crossed Wood River, went a little farther and stopped for noon[.] About 1 o'clock went on. We have travelled about 22 miles to-day.

We passed a windmill to-day[.] Something new for our children to see. It has been very windy and cool all day, looks some like rain. Mr. Earp had a chill yesterday, took some medicine and is better to-day.

Tuesday 14th [June]

Last night had quite a thunderstorm with a very light wind, we heard the wind coming fully an hour[.] We happened fortunately to camp near some timber, which broke the wind coming from us[.] It was quite an unpleasant place to camp, being so many mosquitoes[.]

One of our horses was sick this morning which made us have a late start. Saw a great many prairie dogs coming along. Came very near having a sad accident John falling out of Tom's waggon[.]

Travelled about 21 miles to-day[.] It is now raining quite fast. Camped about 3 miles above Ft. Kearney.

Wednesday 15th [June]

Quite a disagreeable morning[,] misting rain most of the time. Greatly disappointed not being able to cross [the] river to Ft. Kearney. The river too high to ford.

One family left us this morning, Mr. McCritty's[.] He did not think his health would permit him to travel any farther at present. We hated to have him leave us and he appeared to hate leaving.

We have traveled about 9 miles this morning, and have now stopped for noon, it has cleared off quite pretty. The country has changed in appearance much[,] being much more hilly and Bluffs on each side of the River[.] By looking through the marine glass on the south side of the river it seems there must be a hundred teams at least[.] The children brought quite a number of Prickly Pears to let me see.

We have now passed all civilization. We traveled o nto Elm Creek and have camped for the night[.] It has been a very unpleasant day raining off and on all the time, the dust is now laid pretty well. We are now in the Buffalo

Country. We have seen a great number of heads on the Plains[,] some very large ones. Traveled 21 miles to-day.

Mr. Earp got on horse back this morning to hunt us a good camping place, and as he was coming back he saw a big log burning at a little distance so he went to see what it was, to see if some had been camping there, and sure enough some one had camped there and burned up a man[.] There were his bones. We suppose one had been murdered and they burned him up[.] It was close [to] where we camped.

Thursday 16th [June]

This morning cloudy and cool, the birds singing merrily[,] "Oh how sweet the sounds of birds."

The 1864 Diary of Mrs. Sarah Jane Rousseau

We have again started on a long journey, the weather is very unpleasant to-day, misting rain most of the time. We have crossed over three deep ravines this morning, the last one was the worst being almost perpendicular.

We have now stopped to noon, it has cleared off rather pleasant. I hope we shall have some clear dry weather now. Our travel to-day has been through a good many mud holes.

We had quite a scare this morning. Little Oscar Hamilton[2] was riding on horseback when his horse took fright at something and ran off with him at full speed[,] passing our train and him screaming as loud as he could yell[.] The men tried to stop the horse but could not[.] The little fellow managed to get his leg over and

---

[2] Sarah's inclusion is only record of Oscar Hamilton's existence.

held onto the saddle and dropped himself down[.] And[,] as good luck would have it, it happened to be a mud hole where he fell[,] so he escaped unhurt.

We went some farther and stopped to noon at Buffalo Creek, being some 14 miles. Traveled 8 miles more and camped on West side of Buffalo Creek, grass quite scarce, plenty of wood and water.

Traveled 22 miles to-day.

[**Margin entry reads:** June the 16th 220 miles.]

Friday 17th [June]

Another cloudy cool morning. I think we will have more rain. Misted and rained some[.]

We had somewhat hard driving[,] so many bad mud holes, then we had to cross over so many sandy Bluffs[.] Our train of horse teams have increased considerably to-day, making in all I believe 20 waggons, besides the Ox teams[.] There is a great many more Ox teams than horse teams.

It cleared off pretty and warm this afternoon. We have travelled about 20 miles to-day and have now camp for the night,[.]

East fourteen miles from Skunk Creek, the mosquitoes are very bad. Tonight it has clouded over again.

Mr. Earp saw 2 antelopes this morning, they crossed the road about ¼ of a mile ahead of us. Mr. Earp took aim and fired[,] wounding one of them[.] The wounded one got up and they ran off. They followed them a while, but did not get up with them.

[**Margin entry reads:** June 17th 234 miles]

Saturday 18th [June]

Another cloudy disagreeable morning[,] misting rain. It has cleared off and very warm.

We passed by a grave this morning close by the road, a good many of them got out to look at it. It was the grave of a little boy about the size of Albert. He was killed by the Indians last month, name not intelligible[.] We have passed a good many graves, it is indeed a melancholy sight, a good many of them supposed to have been killed by carelessness in allowing children to ride in front of a four horse team, they get tired out and [fall].

We have camped for noon, not very good grass. I suppose we have travelled about 10 miles this morning[.] It is exceedingly warm[.] We can see a very large train on the South side of the river.

Traveled this afternoon over a good many low Sandy Bluffs down to the river where we watered our horses and went on about a mile farther and camped on the North side of the river, grass and water close by some Bluffs.

We are now in the Sioux Indian country. We feel afraid to go out of the sight of our train. When Indians don't feel friendly they don't show themselves but hide behind the Bluffs. I feel a good deal afraid. We may have trouble with them.

To-day I think has been the warmest I ever felt, it seems as though we could hardly bear it[.] After we camped[,] a cloud arose and threatened a storm, but I think it will go round as it has cleared considerably[.]

We are now 275 miles from Omaha.

[**Margin entry reads:** June 257 miles]

Sunday 19th [June]

A pleasant morning[,] bids fair to be a very warm to-day[.] Last night was splendid, cleared off, cool and pleasant, the moon shining bright[.]

We travelled about 8 miles this morning and stopped to noon[.] After dinner[,] went three miles and crossed skunk Creek, went on 7 miles farther, where we found a good spring of cold water at the foot of this Bluffs, North of the rode at the head of the Pawnee Swamps.

Where we camped the water is excellent, which we partook of rather bountifully having had bad water so long[.] To-day was very warm, we suffered and the horses too with the heat[.] We traveled to-day in all 18 miles.

[**Margin entry reads:** June 19th 293 miles]

Monday 20th [June]

The 1864 Diary of Mrs. Sarah Jane Rousseau

Pleasant and warm[.] Came to the conclusion this morning to lay over and wash, as we were at such a good camping place, plenty of grass and water but no wood. We prepared ourselves for that[.] We hauled enough wood to do our washing and cooking so we felt safe.

The girls have been washing all the morning. It is a tremendous warm day[.] This is the third day it has been so excessively warm, the last two days was so warm, clouded up about sun down and threatened a storm, but it cleared off quite pretty and pleasant. I greatly fear one of those awful storms they are apt to have on the plains after such very warm weather.

There was a sad accident occurred this morning. A young man that was driving a team in another train camp close by us, went along with some others to get some wood on an island in the river and got drowned[.] The poor fellow had no relatives or friend along. Mr. Earp tried to get his body but the current was too swift.

I was cupped in three places on my back. I have suffered considerably with my back the last week or two. It has been exceedingly warm to-day. As usual[,] about sundown[,] a cloud arose and it thundered a few times, but it cleared off and we had a beautiful sight.

[**Margin entry reads:** Laid over]

Tuesday 21st [June]

A warm morning, pretty and clear and still. About ready to make another start.

After we rode about a couple of hours we saw several ox teams coming. The men went to see what they were coming back for. They found out they were Mormons.

We passed another grave this morning. A young man 24 years, killed by the Indians on the 23 of May. Passed two more graves this afternoon[,] one an old man 64[,] the other a babe half an hour old. I had no idea we would pass by so many graves.

Stopped to camp.

[**Margin entry reads:** Traveled 17 miles to-day 310]

Wednesday 22nd [June]

A pretty cool morning. Passed Black Mud Creek. Small Creek, Steep banks, very little water. Crossed North Bluff fork. 6 rods wide and 2 feet deep. Sandy Bluffs West foot. Sandy Bluffs East foot.

[**Margin entry reads:** Moved 319. Traveled 18 miles to-day 328]

Thursday 23rd [June]

Jesse Curtis['] waggon broke down just as we got over the Bluffs. We are now detained till he gets it mended. The Bluffs are hard for the horses and mules to go over.

There are a great many Sioux Indians on the south side of the River. I feel afraid [of] them as they are not disposed to feel friendly. We heard there is four thousand of them at Ft. Laramie.

It has taken half a day to get Jesse's axel tree mended. We went on six miles crossing over Bluff Creek running between the Bluffs where we have camped[.]

Traveled 10 miles to-day.

[**Margin entry reads:** Traveled this morning about 3 miles. Traveled 10 miles to-day making 338.]

Friday 24 [June]

A pleasant morning. It blowed hard all night and was quite cool. Mattie has had a bad headache for three days. Yesterday she had a chill, took medicine last night. Not up yet[,] I don't know how she is.

Mattie is some better to-day, having only a slight chill and some fever. Started went to Bluff Spring. Land swampy and soft.

Came to Goose Creek. 30 feet wide and three inches deep. Low range of Bluffs, Sandy one fourth mile wide. Many Springs of cold water at the foot of the Bluffs. Small Creek four feet wide. Shoal Creek three feet wide. Rattle Snake Creek. Twenty feet wide and 18 inches deep. This is the first time we have used

Buffalo Chips to finish getting our supper. It does tolerable well when we can't get anything else.

The Indians are driving the Buffaloes and all the game off. We have not seen live Buffalo yet. Only two antelopes which they tried to kill and could not.

[A] more miserable desolate looking country I never saw. Sandy Barren looking Bluffs. Only a little ridge of bottom land that looks tillable. The Platte River is rather pretty stream being filled with a number of Islands both small and large.

We have traveled about 20 miles to-day.

[**Margin entry reads:** Traveled 358]

Saturday 25 [June]

A pleasant morning and very warm. The days are exceedingly warm.

Started this morning and crossed Camp Creek. Eight feet wide. A little farther on[,] two creeks about the same size, and camped for noon. When a storm came in double quick this time such as I have dreaded all the time since we came on the Platte. It Blowed, Hailed, Rained, Thundered and Lightened. Our horses took fright and ran off. We did not know where.

After the storm was over[,] the Dr. and several others started after them. There was four of our horses gone and four that belonged to another man[.] They were very lucky in finding them. Ours had gone about 7 miles and stopped to grase, the others went onto a pack train[.] The men stopped them and tied them up. They got them all and got back before dark. I felt truly glad to see them come. I don't wish to see such another time. And the curtains on our carriage is cut considerably. A good many of them staked their waggons to keep them from going over.

Traveled 10 miles to-day.

[**Margin entry** reads: 368 miles]

Sunday 26th [June]

This morning cloudy.

Made another start. Crossed Wolf Creek twenty feet wide. Crossed some high Sandy Bluffs[.]

Putting 2 mule teams with our own two teams, and they had to stop a good many times going up.

We passed another new made grave. It was a boy 18 years old that was killed by a horse stampede. The horses running over him. It seems shocking to see so many graves. So many killed. It makes me so much afraid of these hard storms on the Plains. It looks like we might have another one this week evening. It is so warm.

Passed Watch Creek. Went on farther and camp close by the River. A very poor camping place. The ground full of poison. A good many alkalie holes and poor grass. Fastened our carriage down. The wind pretty high[,] thought we might have a storm tonight but it went over.

Traveled about 12 miles to-day.

Monday 27th [June]

A tolerable warm morning. Started to go to Ash Hollow. Next Castle Creek. Then Castle Bluffs, which had a rather romantic appearance but not as much as I thought it would. Sand Hill Creek.

It has been exceedingly warm to-day. Every appearance of a storm cloud arose and the wind blowed tolerably strong. We staked our waggon, but fortune favoured us. It went around.

The 1864 Diary of Mrs. Sarah Jane Rousseau

We traveled about 25 miles to-day.

Tuesday 28th [June]

A very warm morning. Traveled over Dry Creek. Crab Creek twenty feet wide. Went on some farther and stopped for noon. It is tremendous warm. I greatly fear a storm this afternoon.

Traveled by a Dry Lake. Went over Calb's Hills. Passed by some Ancient Bluffs resembling the ruins of Ancient Castle. I thought some of them a pretty good resemblance.

Traveled about 18 miles to-day. Cleared off quite a pretty evening.

Wednesday 29th [June]

A very cool delightful morning. The men are going this morning after some wood. We have had to use drift sticks and willow and some Buffalo Chips which we don't like very well. When they came back with the wood[,] they concluded they had better not go till tomorrow[,] so the girls have been cooking all the afternoon.

The Dr. and Mr. Parker have gone to look at Castle Bluffs to view some of the romantic. It has clouded over[,] looks like it might rain tonight.

Thursday 30th [June]

Cloudy morning, has the appearance of rain. Heard the wolves last night and night before.

It has cleared off now and the sun shines bright. Started again. Traveled a few miles. Looked through the Marine Glass and saw Chimney Rock, south side of the river. It is about 25 miles from here.

Passed a new made grave, it was a man killed by the Indians on the 24th. I suppose he had strayed from the train and got killed.

We are now camped. It is the prettiest camping place we have had for some time. Close by the road and very pretty scenery all around. Plenty of good grass and splendid evening. The wolves were howling [at] us last night and the night before.

We have traveled some 22 miles to-day.

Friday July 1st

A pleasant morning rather cool. Last night after we had been in bed some time[,] the Dr. was told to get up as there was a big storm approaching[.] The wind was blowing real hard. He got up and staked our waggon down. Went to the tent and called the children up and they came in the waggon bringing their beds and all we all slept in the carriage together. It thundered, lightened and rained a pretty smart shower, but it did not hail.

We had to lay over to-day on account of one of our horses being so lame and the girls thought they would wash up the dirty clothes. The men[,] a good many of them[,] have gone hunting. It is a very nice day, but very warm.

Saturday 2nd [July]

A cloud came up last evening before retiring and felt some afraid of a storm. We had our carriage staked and the tent besides having it staked round the bottom as secure as possible. Had ropes fastened to the top and tied to the waggon.

About midnight I should suppose[,] it came in good [and] earnest, blowing dreadfully hard. And heavy thunder & lightened. I raised up in bed and rest myself[,] not knowing we would be capsised. But it did not hail, only rained and that not as hard as I thought it would. But thanks to a merciful God. For his tender care and mercies towards us.

This morning very cool and cloudy, has the appearance of rain. Getting ready to start.

Been cool all day and cloudy[,] until this evening[,] it has cleared off real pretty. Travelled about 10 miles this morning and stopped to noon.

We passed several waggons just before noon and when we stopped[,] the Indians came to us. We had quite a time with them. They had skins to sell and Moccasins. We bought 1 skin and we gave a dollar and a quarter, the other one a cup of sugar and bought John a pair of moccasins which we paid for in meat. They appeared very friendly.

We camped near the river. It is a pretty evening and clear. The wind blows pretty brisk. You can easily see this country is subject to hard storms. The Bluffs show it by their appearance. I shall be glad when we get through this part of the country. Still it is pretty and shows the picturesque.

Our horse Charlie is still very lame. Traveled some 18 miles to-day. We are nearly opposite Chimney Rock.

Sunday 3rd [July]

A pretty clear warm morning. Oh that we may spend the Sabbath as near right as we can under present circumstances. Charlie is very lame yet. We are getting ready to start but don't know how far we can travel.

Traveled this morning about 10 miles. Stopped for noon. It is excessively warm.

I have just been taking a view of Scotts Bluff through the Marine Glass. Tis a splendid sight I can picture while looking a little back. A Gothic looking Edifice like a church with windows and doors and as it were a couple of individuals one in the doorway. The other a little one side and on the left hand[,] it seems as if there is two more coming down a slope to the church, and both on the right and left hand, large Gothic looking ruins. It does really look splendid. The sun as it shines at the present time gives it the right kind of appearance.

About ready to make another start. Went about 5 miles and came to Spring Creek, where we camped.

Traveled about 20 miles to-day. 476 miles[.]

Monday 4th [July]

A pleasant morning. I think it would be a pretty day. Had to lie over on account of Charlie's feet. He is very lame.

The girls went to the Bluffs to-day with Em Curtis, Richard Curtis and Mr. Parker to take a view of the surrounding country. They said it was a pretty sight. At night we had a speech from Thomas Ellis and Jesse Curtis and finished the 4th of July with a dance.

Tuesday 5th [July]

A foggy morning bids fair to be a warm day. Dick Curtis is sick this morning. The Dr. gave him some medicine.

Passed over this morning a desolate barren region of county. Seemingly not fit for man or beast. Very poor grass and little of it. Came by about 20 wigwams, and as a matter of course[,] there are plenty of natives. The Dr. bought half a Buffalo skin from them which he gave 2 dollars for to make shoes for Charlie.

This afternoon passed quite a village of Indians. I suppose there was at least 40 wigwams. I can't tell how many Indians. They make a curious appearance. Some about naked. And some dressed up in thick Buffalo skins while others have some kind of a shirt or old dress. They seem friendly but they are treacherous. We heard this afternoon[,] four nights ago[,] there was a whole train lost all their horses, some 40 of them, I don't know how we will fare.

For 50 miles there will be considerable danger. There is some other tribe of Indians, Black Foot. These are the Sioux Indians that we are among now.

We are camped near the River. We had a sight of Laramie Peak to day. On the North side[,] low sandy Bluffs drifted by the wind. 488 miles.

Wednesday 6th [July]

A cool pleasant morning, nothing disturbed us last night.

We have to keep close guard every night. Last night a wind arose and it blew pretty hard. The Dr. got up and staked our waggon down. I hope we shall be out of reach of these dreadful storms before a great while.

Mattie had quite a sick spell yesterday afternoon and took medicine last night and feels a good deal better this morning.

Started on our journey again. Travelled about [missing] miles and stopped to noon. But found there was no grass, so we went on.

Two groups of Indians passed by us at a small distance which showed they were not friendly. When they feel friendly[,] they will come round your waggons or tents.

This has been a very unpleasant day, the wind blowing very hard. It is a perfect sandy desert that we traveled over to day. The sand blowing in our eyes almost putting them out. We are in Idaho, got here last evening. It looks an awful desolate country at present we are camped close by the river at an Indian Missionary Station.

Traveled 17 miles to-day. 510 miles Idaho territory July 6 1864.

Thursday 7th [July]

This morning cold enough for frost.

We were not disturbed last night by the Indians. They appeared friendly. I suppose to-day will take us where there is more to be feared by them. We are now where there is plenty of wild currents[,] the first fruit we have seen. Our little boys went and got some yesterday evening, they are very large and the skin is tough on them.

The Indians here have rather a strange way of burying their dead. They have four sticks about 10 to 12 feet high and they placed their dead on top of them, it has a very singular appearance.

Having travelled about 6 miles this morning brought as opposite Ft. Laramie. The Dr. has gone across to Laramie to see if there is any letters for us. He has come back brought 2 letters with him.

Laramie has quite a picturesque appearance from this side. There is a good many Indians around. But we have not been disturbed by them.

Traveled 13 miles to-day. 522.

Friday 8 [July]

We came pretty near having an unpleasant time last night. We have to keep close watch day at night over the stock. Mr. Earp went to see about the guards and he found they had got up a dance. And he told them they must quit their dancing and be on duty.

One of the soldiers told him to mind his own business and ordered him off. It made him awful mad and he was for killing. He used very profane language he could hardly be appeased. But he cooled down after a while and all was quiet.

This morning is pleasant and warm. Crossed Dry Creek. We are camped close by a blacksmith. We have to stay and have some work done. We want to get away as soon as possible. The Blacksmith has a squaw for a wife. They are dreadfully low set.

The 1864 Diary of Mrs. Sarah Jane Rousseau

Started between 10 and 11 o'clock passed over some dreadful bad roads, rocky and broken. We had some very high hills to go over.

The scenery was grand, bordering on Romantic. One high hill towering above another in their majestic appearance. But worst of all was the wind, which blew a fair hurricane all the afternoon. The dust and sand almost putting our eyes out.

We had to keep pretty close together as the Indians are bad about stealing horses. There is a man that was about 100 yards behind the rest not thinking of danger when some Indians came from behind the Bluffs, and took his four mules out of his waggon and ran them off. He was too far from his train to get assistance. There is every opportunity to run them off, run them over the Bluffs and nobody could tell where they went.

Well we traveled until we got to the river[,] which was after sun down considerably. Watered our horses but could not find any feed for the stock as it was too dark to see. The poor horses was tired and hungry. We had a little meal that we mixed with some flour and water. Some would eat it and some would not so we correled, being as close together with possible, fastening the horses inside the Correle to the waggons and kept close guard all night. The wind still blowing very hard.

Traveled this afternoon about 13 miles. 540 miles.

Saturday 9th [July]

A pretty clear morning up quite early, harnessed up and started without breakfast and went about 3 or 4 miles when we came up with a train we had been in company with before.

We [didn't] know at first, but it might be the train the Indians had taken all their horses and left them a few days before, but it turned out to be the New York train we had got acquainted with some time back. They told us they had been laying over as they had found good grass, and plenty of it, and glad we were to hear it.

So here we have camped. While the stock are enjoying their bountiful repast. But the Indians are around. The men are guarding them. All well armed. The men have seen 5 or 6 of them, they are on horseback with their guns on their shoulders. We know they are hostile because they keep aloof.

Traveled between 3 or 4 miles to-day.

Sunday 10th [July]

A beautiful clear, still morning. Where we are camped we're surrounded by high Bluffs. And sand for a carpet. There was nothing interrupted last night.

Started and came about 8 miles. To the right of the road we saw as we thought it at first a number of indian ponies, but it turned out to be emigrants, a great many of their company. We turned in and camped there ourselves as there was over 20 miles of bad mountainous roads and very poor prospect of getting good grass for our horses.

Here[,] there was plenty good grass and water and we did our washing[,] Sunday as it was. Oh it was a great deal against my feeling to have such things done but it seemed unavoidable. I hope e'r long we will get to the end of our journey.

Our trip has been made exceedingly unpleasant on account of Tom Ellis, his continued profanity whenever he was near. A more wicked man I never saw, and one more ungentlemanly. I believe he will leave this morning as Mattie won't do his washing anymore, he has treated her so unmanly cursing her all the time.

We passed Alder Creek this morning where there was [a] good spring[.] We watered our horses and got some for ourselves.

Travelled about 8 miles to-day.

Monday 11th [July]

A very pleasant morning, getting ready to make another start. Tom Ellis has gone with another family by the name of Clark. He got mad because Mattie would not do his washing. It has been the most pleasant day I have spent since I left home. We have heard no swearing. All has been quiet and pleasant.

The girls had to do the men's work. The doctor is pretty tired tonight. We must try and get someone else to go with us.

We have traveled over some rough roads to-day and we are now campt close to the River, a very pretty place. It is a pleasant evening, but quite windy.

Traveled to-day about 13 miles. 567 miles.

Tuesday 12th [July]

It is another pleasant morning. It is often when there is sorrow at night[,] "There is joy in the morning." It is even so with us at this time.

Last night after driving our horses across the river to feed[,] some one gave the alarm that Indians were around and that a gentleman in a train close by had just lost three of his horses[,] all that he had. He saw them cut the ropes they were fastened with and ran them off before they could get assistance. Well it caused a good deal of alarm.

They sent the word over the river to the guards that the Indians were about and they all commenced right away to gather up their teams to bring them back and form a correle and fasten the horses inside. The Dr.'s horses were all on the other side, consequently he had no horse to go after them. And he left them to those who were going after theirs to bring his[.] There being so many of them to bring, it took them till dark before they got them over and ours were left behind.

As a matter of course[,] I felt afraid they would be run off by the Indians. But a gentleman by the name Parker that is in our train came over, he was one of the guards[,] and said he left our horses all there a few minutes before and intended going back for them. Mr. Parker acted the part of a gentleman and friend to us which I shall always remember with gratitude. The word came in the mean time, the horses could not be seen anywhere. We supposed immediately they had been run off by the Indians.

I can hardly describe, between hope and despair, hoping they might possibly be feeding somewhere and we could get them and then despairing of our ever getting them again. Then Messrs. Parker, Curtis and Hamilton went over to see if they could get them. But it was too dark for them to see and they stayed all night & in the morning good fortune smiled on us[.] They found them and brought them back.

Oh how rejoiced I felt when they were all safe and we had them.

Well we started on again with joyful hearts[,] passed over some very rough roads and got to the river, being some 9 miles where we stopped for noon. We had hardly got our horses out to eat when the alarm was given the indians were on us[.] Every man was for his gun and revolver and try and catch their horses as there was a regular stampede all running in every direction. Tom Ellis had left us a day or two before and we couldn't get another hand at present. The Dr. and the girls and our little boys were all we had to see to ours.

The indians made a rush by on the Bluffs, our men firing on them as they passed. Oh what an exciting time, the bullets flying in every direction and horses running as hard as they could. I was left alone in the carriage, the rest of them all helping. It is impossible to describe my feelings at such a time and place in this situation I was. Helpless.

They run four of our horses off and five of Mr. Hamilton's and phily belonging to Mr. Curtis. As soon as possible they formed a corelle. The Dr. and all the married gentleman staid to get all the waggons in Corelle while the rest were looking after the horses. They made the Corelle large enough to put the horses in when they should be brought up. It was very laborious work.

Another gentleman came in after us, belonging to another train, was unhitching his horses.

They were taken with their harness on. Here we are in a wilderness several hundred miles from civilization not enough team to go on with, and don't know how long it may be before the rest of them may be taken. Oh how desolate my feelings under such circumstances.

This gentleman held a consultation to see if they could had better follow them up[.] It took some time before they could decide, at last they decided that ten of them should get their horses and arm themselves, and follow after them. One of the gentleman that had three of his horses taken in the harnesses shot his horse accidentaly with his revolver and had to turn back with it.

The party came back at dark without our horses, hearing about them at the train we left at our camping place in the morning. They said if they had been half an hour sooner they could have got them as the indians had just gone past with them on the other side of the river. They had intended crossing there but happened to see their train and they went farther down to cross.

We will have to try and make some arrangement to go on. I think it likely we can get two yoke of oxen to put ours on our big waggon and get a driver and let the horses go as we think it is very unlikely we shall ever get to see them if we should go after them.

Wednesday 13th [July]

This is a pretty bright morning. I feel very sad. But still I am thankful that it is no worse. I will still put my trust in our Heavenly Father who is ever watchful over all his creatures.

Left camp rather late. Traveled over a desolate wilderness. I think I never saw a more barren broken apparently worn out country in my life. Hilly rough sand instead of rich Idaho. I feel more like saying "Oh dear Oh[.]"

I feel disappointed in the appearance of the country. I expected to have seen a rich beautiful country. And no doubt but there is beauty and richness in Idaho, but we have not seen it as yet.

Our appearance in the train to-day seems rather strange. Instead of our four pretty horses we have 2 yoke of oxen, which we were glad to get so that we could proceed in our journey.

We traveled about 10 miles to-day. 567 miles.

Thursday 14th [July]

A pleasant morning. Traveled steep and craggy ascent. Road mountainous. Came to the river and watered our horses[.] Intended nooning but found that there was no grass so we went on some farther, found a little grass and camped.

After we started this morning, we saw a number of Indians on the opposite side of the river. They had stampeded some horses and were taking them off. All the men got their guns and revolvers, thinking we were going to be attacked. The Dr. and Mr. Tucker started on foot toward the River to see if they could get a shot at them. They followed on by the river a good way. Mr. Tucker fired on them. When they had got back to the train, they said if they had been on horseback they could have crossed the river and got the horses. The indians and horses seemed tired down.

We are in the most dangerous part of the country. They have seen them following us up fifty or sixty miles. The guards went along side of the trail all day.

We passed some dangerous roads to-day for an attack high Cliffs on both sides. We had to be very watchful.

As soon as we were camped[,] they put the stock out to feed[.] Had plenty of guards out watching. They had not been out over a couple of hours, when the alarm was given the indians were on us. Our men were prepared to follow them. They came as before[,] full speed to stampede our horses, but we were ready and headed them. But still they appeared determined to make a rush on us by circling around a little.

Several of the men by this time caught a horse and took their guns and followed after them at full speed[,] firing at them as they went. One of the men who is in our company was a little ahead of this rest[,] and in the attempt of firing at the indians killed his own horse from under him which left him to the mercy of the enemy. Luckily our men were close at hand and saved him from the dreadful fate that awaited him.

The Indians turned on them and they had a regular fight[.] They shot their bows and arrows[.] The men brought 2 of them back with them.

The Dr. was one of the men that went on horseback after them[.] He recognized one of the Indians we bought some elk skins from,[3] and which appeared the most friendly kind. But they are treacherous. He also saw a white man that he saw the other side of Laramie and

---

[3] See July 2 or 3.

wanted to trade horses with him Charlie being some lame, he said we wouldn't be able to carry him through. The Dr. the instant he saw him told the men to shoot him as he was a white man. He heard him he supposed as he made a quick move to get out of the way. They fired a good many shots but did not know if they hit him. Our men scared them off completely. They returned no more.

The Sioux Indians displayed a great deal of daring and bravery. They make a dash among the whites seemingly not caring for anything, stampede the horses and take them off.

When they came this time[,] two of the women came and gave us their babies to take care of, they screaming poor little things as loud as they could yell. The women having to run and catch the horses while the men are keeping the indians off.

It is indeed an exciting time and still I can't account for my feelings. I fear that I am getting some stoical. I sit in the waggon and see all that is going on and it don't appear to move me. (I won't say that neither for I must acknowledge I feel afraid some of the time.)

We have made some 13 miles to-day. 581 miles.

Friday 15th [July]

Rather cool and cloudy morning. It rained and blew hard in the night[,] rained some this morning.

Made rather a late start this morning. Traveled over some high, rolling, barren country. Stopped to noon.

The Dr. had just gotten his horses out to feed when the news was that Mrs. Hamilton was sick. We moved our waggon about a mile farther to get good grass for horses[,] formed a corelle and raised or tents. Mrs. Hamilton had a fine son about a couple of hours after we camp.

We have just heard them say the indians were in sight. I hope they will not come up on us to-night.

As we were riding along to-day Mattie saw a stake with a paper attached to it. She got out to see what it could be. There was written on it be careful here, one man was shot all to pieces, and horses run off. I hope when we get to the Ferry of the Platte there will not be so much danger. This is where the Telegraph stops.

We have come about 10 miles to-day. 590 miles.

Saturday 16th [July]

I again hear the sweet music of birds. This morning bright and clear.

Last night nothing occurred to disturb our sweet repose. Though danger surrounds us on every side[,] a kind and Merciful God watched over us and protected us. "Oh let us praise his Great and Holy name."

We are detained here to-day on account of Mrs. Hamilton. All this still, no sound of any indians, the women are most all engaged, some washing some cooking. Mattie washed to-day and Elizabeth is doing the cooking.

About 4 o'clock this afternoon the men thought they saw some indians coming. We saw plainly there were some horsemen on the other side of the river, but could not discover yet whether they were indians or white men. The Dr. and a good many other men gathered on the bank with their guns to be ready in case of emergency. The Dr. looked through the Marine glass and discovered them to be soldiers. The next fear was they might be spies, but they told them to come across which they did. They had come to stop the train from leaving the camp until further orders, as the Indians had been committing great depredations among the emigrants.

The soldiers said they had killed 14 men and captured three women and one child, and two men they wounded. The Lieut. was a surgeon and he said he dressed the wounds of the men. He said the indians were getting so bad. He received word by telegraph the night before, they had to go and stop the trains from going from camp till further orders.

The Lieut. and his soldiers took supper with us. The Lieut. appeared to be a very pleasant man. He enquired if we had lost any horses. Dr. told him 4[.] Before the soldiers left they said we might move in the morning, but not to go any farther than 20 miles, till we heard from them.

July 17th [July]

Passed last night without being disturbed. It is a very pretty looking morning.

Started from camp about 6 o'clock[.] When we had gone a short distance we saw a paper staked to the ground. Mattie got out to see what it was. It stated that the Oliver train had lost 8 head of horses[,] no lives lost, but had a very narrow escape. And we heard another train that they call the Batcheler had 25 head of horses taken the day after we lost ours. We saw another written paper that told of a man being found dead killed by the Indians he had several arrows shot through him.

We went on till we came to the soldier station. There we heard that one of the captured women made her escape from the Indians and had just arrived there. She caught one of their ponies and had rode two days and nights without anything to eat. We don't know how reliable that statement is as we did not see the woman.

The Dr. has gone back there this morning to see about John's mare. We heard that the train behind us had taken up two horses which answered the descriptions of John['s] mare and one of Mr. Hamilton[']s. I hope it is true. The Lieut. said the night before last they thought of getting two or three hundred soldiers, and what man they could from the different trains, and go to their Indian Village[,] take all the horses and clean them all out. It is supposed there can[']t be less than a thousand horses stolen.

The 1864 Diary of Mrs. Sarah Jane Rousseau

We are now camped 2 miles from the Soldiers station. A more broken desolate sandy wilderness I never saw. There is a train just passed by, and in one of the waggons there is a man the indians had shot their arrows in three different places. He said he was driving his own team ahead of the train some little distance and that was the cause of being attacked.

We traveled to-day about 12 miles.

[**Editorial note:** The full extent of robberies and lives lost during the attacks from July 12-14 are found in the book, *Emigrant Tales of the Platte River Raids* (2023).]

Monday 18th [July]

The Dr. got back but did not bring the horses. They told him the train had not come up yet, likely they would be here to-day some time.

Some are anxious to start again as soon as dinner is over. After all the warning the soldier had given them. Two soldiers have just gone by riding as hard as they could to stop the train that has gone ahead.

I think it presumptuous for us to go on yet, as we were told not to go. It is said there is 2000 indians above, the Sioux and the Comanche. The most wicked and bloodthirsty Indians we have. it seems that we are in a very dangerous situation. We cannot tell what will become of us all.

The Dr. went again this evening to see if the train had come but it had not, we fear they are in some trouble with the indians. The Dr. said when he returned that we might go on. The Lieut. said the order had been countermanded. That we could have would have to defend ourselves. I suppose we will make another start on our perilous journey in the morning.

Tuesday 19th [July]

Cloudy and rather cool this morning. It blew hard in the night, and still blowing a brisk breeze[.] Preparing to start as soon as breakfast is over.

Started from camp about six o'clock. After traveling a short distance we got somewhat of a fright[.] Some of the men thought they saw indians coming. We hurried and formed a corelle while Mr. Earp went on the Bluff to see if they were coming. He viewed all around and beckoned us to go on. It was a false alarm and we were glad it was.

John came running to our waggon and said his mare had come[.] He said two men rode up on horseback and one of the horses was his mare, the other was Mr. Hamilton's. We were very glad to get them back.

The men said when they first saw horses, they were going back as fast as they could, they need to be scared pretty near to death, starting at anything could see or hear. If we could only get the other three we would feel made up, but I suppose we will never get them again.

Wednesday 20th [July]

Quite cloudy this morning[.] Rained considerable in the night. Another train came up last night, corelled close by us, the same train our horses were in.

I think we will all join into one train as we hear there is so much danger with the Indians. If we do[,] there will be about 100 waggons. I think there will be enough then to defend ourselves.

We heard there was a large train on the south side of the river. They had the finest looking horses and mules that had gone along this spring. They had sixty heads stolen from them[,] was only Indians that did all that mischief, they got some four back. I believe the Indians got 43 three of them.

The indians[,] when they go on such an expedition[,] are strapped to their ponies, they can't fall off if they even get killed. The Lieut. told the Dr. to kill every one of them that came about, friend or foe.

There was one poor fellow lost his life with what they call a friendly indian[.] He came around asking for bread, when the man turned round to get him some[,] the indian shot him dead. When I think how often we have done the same thing, and might have shared the same fate, it makes me feel dreadful.

Nothing disturbed by repose last night. We traveled over some rough looking country to day. A barren, desolate looking wilderness, and to add to our comfort we got into a nest of flying ants. I never saw such swarms in my life. It seemed as if they would take everything. The horses and our cattle seemed as if they would go crazy with them. At least at last we got out of their reach.

We went on until the middle of the afternoon. Stopped to water our horses and then came to the conclusion to stay over night. A cloud arose about sundown which threatened a coming storm. At last it came just before we got our supper cooked, it thundered, lightened blowed & rained very hard, we had to get our supper the best we could and went to bed, all of us sleeping in the two waggons not being able to get up.

Thursday 21st [July]

Started from camp this morning without eating breakfast[,] there being not enough grass for this stock to feed on. Went onto the upper Platte ferry and ford. There, we met a gentleman that traveled in a train that left us below Laramie, his name is Northrop. We did not meet him again until this morning.

There was two families that traveled in a train. One of them named Morse the other Wright. They left our train at Laramie to go to the South side of the river. Mr. Northrop told us this morning the indians had killed Mr. Wright.

We used to call him Buck Skin as he wore buckskin breeches fringed down the side.

I felt real sorry to hear the poor fellow was killed. He did not appear to be afraid of anything. Mr. Morse, the man Mr. Wright was going with, rode about a mile ahead of the train, while Mr. Wright rode on horseback besides them. An indian came to the waggon and asked for bread. Morse laid down his gun to get him some when the indian took up Morse's gun and fired at him. Immediately about thirty Indians made their appearance. They surrounded Wright and fired three shots at him[;] one through his heart, another in his back and one in his leg.

Meanwhile Morse's wife took the lines[,] turned as quick as thought[,] and went back as hard as she could to the train while her husband was throwing the things out of the waggon to lighten it.

It is awful to think of the depredations and mischief the indians have done this season.

We heard of one small train completely destroyed. The people all massacred and waggons burned. They found the body of a little girl. They had shot several arrows in her, tomahawked, and scalped her.

Got ready for another start when we found out our cattle was gone, hunted around but could not see nothing of them[.] Went down to the river with our horse team to water, leaving our big waggon back on the hill.

The Dr. went back to see if all was right and returned pretty quick saying there was something the matter, but could not tell us what it was, took his gun and went on the hill, and wanted some of the men to follow him as Mr. Earp was running around at a great rate. It was not long before a good many was on horse back with their guns, and several soldiers went as fast as their horses would carry them.

This is a soldier station and where the Telegraph stops and post office. I sent out a letter to Mary Ann here.

The men returned in an hour or so and said there was nothing particular the matter. They saw three indians at a distance, before the men got back it was told Mr. Earp was surrounded by 15 Indians, it alarmed Mrs. Earp very much. She felt certain he would be killed. The Dr. being on foot[,] I was scared a good deal about him, but they all got back safe.

A cloud arose this evening. It blew, rained, thundered, and lightened. Just before dusk[,] two men brought cattle back. They had followed a train that went by. I was glad we found them. Two men rode up before it commenced to rain and asked if some man in the train wanted to buy some horses. They had only one of the horses they wanted to sell with them. The Dr. and Mr. Earp went to their camp to see the other horses. I was afraid for them to go [as] there is so much danger around us, it was pretty near dark when they started.

They returned in a couple of hours quite safe bringing along with them two horses. The Dr.

gave 300 dollars for the two. We now have a four horse team again. I hope we will have better luck than we have had heretofore.

One of Jesse Curtis's cows died yesterday. We don't know what was the matter with it, we are continually seeing dead cattle on the road. I suppose hard driving and little feed and some think drinking alkali is the cause of so many dying.

Friday 22nd [July]

No interruption from the indians last night. A very pleasant morning. Soon ready to make another start. There is a great many trains gone ahead of us.

Went over some rough roads to-day. Stopped for noon close by the river. We passed about a dozen dead cows. The country is mountainous. We are close by the mountain, they called the red Buttes. They have a singular appearance. Travelled about 15 miles to-day.

Saturday 23 [July]

A very delightful morning. Nothing disturbed our sweet repose last night. Our horses had a bountiful repast last night and this morning. I felt so sorry for the poor things, working so hard and having such a scarcity of feed. I hope we will get along now, we have not seen any indian a day or two. I hope we will see no more of them. We are about four miles West of Prospect Hill, Montana Territory.

Traveled over some rough mountainous country to-day, past any amount of dead cattle. Nooned to-day where there was a great deal of alkali, one of our horses was loose and ran to the water to drink took too much and made him sick. It is dangerous for them to drink too much. Got a camping place at dark.

Traveled about 18 miles to-day. (Montana Territory July 23, 1864)

Sunday 24 [July]

Another very pretty morning. Oh Savior[,] help us to spend this day as near right as we can under our present circumstances. Not sinning knowingly or willfully, but remembering it is the Sabbath.

Our horse is better this morning. Pretty near ready to leave camp.

The traveling is a great deal better to-day. The roads much smoother, not much sand. The mountains have an imposing picturesque appearance but the country[,] how desolate and dreary they look. No vegetation. Nothing but wild sage and grease wood, which we use in place of wood to cook with. Grease wood I think a very pretty shrub something similar to cedar.

We are now camped close by what is called Independence Rock, situated on the North side of the river. It is 600 yards long and 120 wide. It is a formable looking Rock composed of hard granite. We are 660 miles from Omaha.

Monday 25th [July]

Another pleasant morning. There is very little grass at this place. We intend leaving as soon as possible to get better grass and lay over two or three days to rest our team. They have pretty near given out.

Passed what is called Devil's Gate. The river here passes between perpendicular rocks 400 feet high. The girls and some others have gone to see wonderful works of nature. I know it must be a grand sight. Oh how I wish I could have made one of the party, but I must submit[.]

The party have returned from their visit to the Devil's Gate and seemed wonderfully pleased with their site. They would not have missed seeing it for anything.

Tuesday 26th [July]

A pleasant morning. Came to the conclusion to go on slowly instead of laying over.

Started and made a pretty good travel, going over some good roads, and some pretty rough. It is a very rough country to say the best. But still the mountains have an imposing and picturesque appearance. The country is desolate in the extreme. It certainly never was intended for any white person to inhabit. Nothing but a wild howling wilderness.

We have come to-day about 22 miles.

We heard to-day, it was telegraphed last evening, the soldiers and Sioux Indians had a fight. The soldiers captured 200 head of horses. I should not be surprised if our horses was some of them.

It is said that the Arrapahoes and Snakes are fighting, above where we are. They have joined to-gether and are fighting the emegrants. I hope we will not come in contact with them.

Wednesday 27th [July]

A beautiful morning, left camp about 6 o'clock. The road this morning was pretty good. The country here is very mountainous, and some of the scenery is very grand. Some of the mountains appear to be perfectly smooth while others close by are very rough, and some almost covered with Pine trees, which give them a very black appearance. They are very high. I suppose some 300 feet, and most all composed of solid granite.

Stopped for noon, found there was no grass and went on farther, found more grass near the Soldier station and stopped. The Dr. and Mr. Hamilton went to the soldier station to see if they could find [out] anything about his horses. The soldiers and Indians had a fight. The soldiers taking two head of horses, and thought they might possibly have ours among them. They thought of telegraphing us and find out if they had seen or heard of them. I believe the conclusion is to go on.

There has been a fight above with the Sioux and Snake Indians. Some say there was 25 Siouxs seen night before last on their return from the fight, they have taken a good many of the Snakes scalps. We greatly feared we would have a good deal of trouble with the Indians above. But a gentleman on his return home, corelled close to us, said he has only saw five squaws, and if there was any trouble with them it was since he passed along. He has been polite enough to take a letter for us to Mary Ann. He lives in Eddyville. His name is Wallace.

Mr. Parker left Mr. Clark and is now traveling along with us. (38 miles West of Devils Gate. Ford #4 good camping place.)

Thursday 28th [July]

Pleasant morning. The wind blew hard last night. It is now calm and serene. We will soon be ready to make another start[.]
Left camp traveled over some rough, and some tolerable good roads. Elizabeth said she saw some high mountains in the distance, asked her Pa if he saw them, he thought it was some high clouds at first, but soon find out if it was the Rock[y] Mountains.

I looked through the Marine glass, it was indeed a splendid sight to behold a mountain[.] it appeared to me in the distance elevated to the Heavens, fringed over with pure white snow. The sun shining on it with all its splendour. I feel utterly incompetent to describe its beauty. If the appearance of it at such a distance is so magnificent how must it look when close by.

All that I passed by, the mountains, Bluffs and all the scenery that I thought looked grand, sinks into nothing[,] into insignificance, in comparison with the splendor of the Rock[y] Mountains. We are some sixty miles distant[.]

We have camped close by the river, rather a pretty place. Travelled about 18 to 20 miles today.

Friday 29th [July]

Clear pretty morning.

Started from camp about 6 o'clock, went over some tolerable smooth road. Stopped for noon close by the river, found very good grass, thought of some of laying over a few days, we desired it very much as our horses[,] poor things[,] were about to give out. It was said about two or three miles farther we would find good grass and water, and the conclusion was we should go that much farther and stop.

We found grass and water aplenty, but the company is divided, some for going on, while others are for staying. The train was stopped. Mr. Earp said he would rather stay as we had some very rough bad roads to go over, and it might happen we would get to good grass and we might not[.] We would have to travel at least ten miles.

We[,] of course[,] were in favor of staying and said so, but the decision was left to Mr. Curtis and he said to go on although he was aware our horses were nearly give out. We felt bad enough about going on, as we thought our horses could hardly be able to travel so far.

Well we started over Rocky Hills, mountainous roads, one of the horses in our waggon gave out and we had to put in another, and poor thing[,] it was not fit to go on but we had to do it.

From some cause, we cannot define, some of those we thought our true friends there appears to be hard feelings, and jealousy existing, whether it is from false tales told around the camp or not I cannot tell. It is one of the best kinds of places for such things.

We get to the end of our hard days travel about sun down, and as we feared little or no grass, our horses worn out and nothing for them to eat. Oh how sorry we feel for the poor things but we could not help ourselves.

A cloud was rising before we got to camp, before we got our horses out it commenced raining pretty smart, a cold disagreeable rain but fortunately it did [last] not a great while. Our camping place is called Strawberry Creek[.]

Traveled to-day about 20 miles.

Saturday 30th [July]

Rather cool and pleasant this morning.

Started a little after sunrise. One man in our train had a sick horse this morning. We suppose yesterday's afternoon drive and not feed enough made him sick, they tried to doctor him some but it did no good, he died about noon.

We are now camping at Willow Creek, fourteen miles from South Pass. Plenty of good grass and water.

Made 6 miles to-day.

Sunday 31st [July]

A freezing cold morning[.]

Left camp about 6 o'clock. Traveled fourteen miles and got to South pass. The famous South

Pass is distant from Ft. Laramie 320 miles, from St. Louis 1,580 and from the mouth of the Columbia 1,400. It is therefore nearly midway between the Mississippi and the Pacific.

The altitude of this wonderful place is 7,490 feet above the level of the sea, and it is from twenty to thirty miles wide. The ascent is so imperceptible that it is not an easy task to acertain the dividing line. A stony ridge crossing the road on the table land is designated as the spot, and its position has been fixed at N. Lat. 42° 20′ and W. Long. 113°.

At the north lies that noble and picturesque chain commonly called Wind River mountains.

On the South is situated Table Mountain, an insignificant chain of low hills.

This day is Sabbath, how unprofitable we have spent it. Mr. Earp got angry with the whole train because they passed him, he took it as an insult, talked pretty hard to all, some thought he had taken a little too much liquor. He used very profane language and told the whole train he would give up his Captaincy unless they would adhere to the rules he gave. After being detained an hour or more[,] very unpleasantly we rolled on[,] all but one family[,] Mr. Clark's. They left.

We are close by some water. It is quite a pretty camping place, plenty of good grass, wood and water. We have a very pretty view of the Rocky Mountains. And I think it is a splendid sight. Every lover of Nature will look at that mountain with wonder and delight. I can truly say I think it one of the most beautiful and grandest pieces of nature's work I ever beheld. Its lofty and elevated appearance with its perpendicular rock some three or four hundred feet high, I should think. The top of the mountains covered with snow gives it a most magnificent appearance. When I look at it[,] it fills my heart with praise and adoration to the Great Creator of all things.

Travelled about 15 miles to-day. We are within 2 miles of the summit.

August. Monday 1st

Quite pleasant this morning, some foggy and rather cool, clouded up rain day pretty smart shower. Cleared off real pretty after while.

Elizabeth washed a large washing, and Mattie did the cooking to-day. We intend laying over a few days to recruit our horses. It clouded over again this afternoon, rained and thundered some, and it is now pretty near cleared off quite pleasant.

Tuesday 2nd [August]

A heavy frost[.] The ground is covered with it. We think of going a mile farther, hitched up and went on a mile or a little upwards and camped. Tolerable good grass, and plenty of wood and water. Took the things out of our waggon and sunned them, the carpet was quite damp in one corner, we laid it on the grass to air.

There is a great plenty of what is called Sage Chickens, they are very nice, they are more like our tame chickens, the meat looks white, not like our prairie hens[,] the meat so dark and strong tasted. The Dr. got three of them to-day, two young ones, we cooked for supper, and I sat in the tent and eat supper with them.

After supper[,] with some help[,] I walked to Mrs. Day's waggon and came back by Mrs. Earp[']s, staid a while with her, and came back to my own home. I think I am improving as fast as I can but still am very helpless. I don't suffer near so much pain as I did a while back.

I thought for a while I wouldn't be able to travel if I didn't get better. I feel now a good deal better, and I have the pleasant anticipation of walking ere long.

Wednesday 3rd [August]

Another cool morning, the ground white with frost. It is now cleared off pretty and warm. The Dr. and Mr. Parker went hunting this morning. We intend making another start in the morning for Salt Lake. We are[,] I believe[,] 250 miles distant.

I don't know how we will get along, our teams are almost give out and we heard there is little or no feed for at least a hundred miles. We thought the intention was to lay over a week or ten days to recruit the teams. Ours need it so much.

Mr. Hamilton's family and some others are anxious to go on and we of course will have to acquiesce in the decision, but I feel afraid we will lose some of our horses by it. The Dr. and Mr. Parker have returned, bringing three sage chickens with them. They said they saw plenty of them, 2 Elks and 6 Antelopes.

[Thursday] August 4th

Another pretty morning cool and white frost. Getting ready for another start[.]

Went from camp about 6 o'clock. Traveled the telegraph rode some few miles, when Mr. Earp saw a road turned to the left. He thought it best that we should turn off to see if we could get good grass for the horses to noon on, but it proved a perfect failure, traveling some miles over a barren wilderness, no vegetation, nothing but wild sage and some grease wood and a few prickly pears.

At last we came to some grass, but could not feed anything off of it. It was covered all over with alkali. We went on to near sun down and stopped for the night. It is a miserable camping place[,] scarcely any grass and what there is mixed with alkali, the water tastes smart of it[.]

Travelled about 15 miles.

Friday 5th [August]

A pleasant bright looking morning, getting ready to start[.]

Traveled over a desert barren looking country, nothing but wild sage and grease wood for the eye to rest on till about noon when we came to what is called Little Sandy, it was quite refreshing to look at this place. A pretty clear stream of good water and plenty of good grass for the stock to regale themselves with, and plenty of fruit[,] gooseberries and currants[.] The boys and girls went out to gather some and had a fine time[.] It is a beautiful place so we formed our corelle, and intend staying till the morning, when we will make another start.

There is considerable game in this part of the country, Elk, Antelope and Sage Chickens. One man in the train killed an Elk to-day and brought the hindquarters home with him, leaving the rest, he could not bring it as he was walking. We had a mess of it for dinner, it was very nice.

Mr. Parker and Richard Curtis went this afternoon to get the other part of it. They have not returned yet, got back about sun down bringing the remaining part of it.

Travelled about 10 miles to-day.

Saturday 6th [August]

A nice morning clear and not very cold. I think it will be a pleasant day.

Started and travelled about 27 miles, this road very smooth and good, going downhill pretty much all the time.

We are now camped by Big Sandy[,] having crossed it twice to-day. Very little grass and what there is [is] mixed considerable with alkali.

Had a good deal of trouble the cattle last night in the corral.

Sunday 7th [August]

This morning pretty and bright. Intend to leave camp as soon as possible to-day and get some grass for our horses to eat[.] Poor things[,] they had very little to eat last night after a long day's ride and the same hard fate this morning[,] nothing to eat.

Got breakfast as early as possible and started again with our poor hungry horses before the rest of the train. Their stock fared a good deal better than our horses. They have some feed for them.

We traveled over to-day some of the most desolate, barren looking country I ever saw, had no idea there was such a wilderness in America. No vegetation save wild sage and grease wood, not a tree or shrub to relieve the eye, so far as your I can reach nothing but sandy bluff and sandy roads to travel over. The telegraph poles[,] we follow along side of them, they appear to me like some old friends.

The 1864 Diary of Mrs. Sarah Jane Rousseau

Well we traveled to-day mile after mile and still no grass. I felt most heartsick to see the poor things going along seemingly they have lost all their ambition for everything, they go along because they are obliged to.

At last we came to Green River[.] Where we have camped[,] plenty of good grass and water. Oh how glad I was when we found such an abundance of it. Green River is a very pretty stream[,] the timber mostly cottonwood and Elm and a good deal of Willow.

After we had camped a few hours our train came up. The Dr. saw them coming through the Marine Glass and went and met them and told them where we were, now we are all together again. I think it likely we will lay over a day or two.

We have come about 12 miles to-day, it was exceedingly warm but it is now cool and pleasant. The Dr. killed a sage chicken this afternoon and we intend having it for supper.

Monday 8th [August]

A pleasant morning[.] Thought it better for us to go on this morning[.]

Started across Green River, got into Utah territory, traveled over some rough desolate, much about the same as we came over yesterday, more rough if any odds and more rocky[.] we are now camped on what is called Black Foot Creek. There appears to have been plenty of grass, but it is all about eat off. We intend making another early start in the morning to find grass for our horses.

The 1864 Diary of Mrs. Sarah Jane Rousseau

Since we camped[,] two or three trains have come which still makes the feed more scarce[.] It has every appearance of rain tonight.

I heard this evening the Indians had been making great depredations among the emegrants on their way to Idaho. Their taking the road that is called Landers Cut Off. There was a train of twelve or thirteen waggons, men taking their families[,] which we heard were all massacred[.] How true it is[,] I do not know.

I have just been looking through the Marine Glass at some mountains covered with snow, it is a very pretty sight. There is more snow on them than any I have seen.

We have traveled to-day about 15 miles.

Tuesday 9th [August]

It rained some last night and the wind blew considerably. This morning is clear and pretty, rather cool, intend leaving camp as soon as possible.

Started by sun up, went over some wild desolate looking country, the roads rough and rocky. Got to Houris fork, watered our horses an filled our kegs, went on to Granger Station.

Here we felt some dubious about proceeding, the road indicating there had been no traveling along, since there had been rain. We were alone with our two waggons and did not know but that we would be attacked by the Indians. We left our train in the morning to hunt grass for the horses, and they had not got up with us as yet, consequently we were alone. The Dr. and Mr. Parker came to the conclusion we had better go on.

After proceeding a few miles we saw the Cummings train coming. On we went[.] Came in sight of some curious looking ruins. As we drew nearer it was indeed an imposing sight. It appeared at first sight like some lofty Castle or Cathedral with its fantastic pillars and high domes. Painted, it appeared to me in different colors, which gave it a beautiful and finished appearance. It was indeed one of Nature's noblest works. I wish I was capable of doing it justice by giving a right description but I will leave it to those who are more imaginative than I am.

We had to go a good distance before we found any grass, thought it doubtful whether we would find any or not. But we fortunately found a little on what is called Black's Fork of Green River, where we have camped for the night.

Traveled 15 miles to-day.

Wednesday 10th [August]

Last night it clouded up, we had quite a brisk wind and some rain. I got out of the waggon myself to night and walked to the tent with the aid of a stick. Oh how thankful I feel to a Merciful God for the restoration of health, may I ever praise his Great and Holy name.

I took a view of the snow capped mountains through the Marine glass last night. It is a most beautiful sight. Though this region of country looks like a barren wilderness yet the wonderful works of nature fills the beholder. The lover of nature in all its splendid works with admiration. We are getting ready to leave camp.

Started rather late this morning, having to make and bake bread for our horses to eat, went on crossed small Creek and some pretty rough rocky road.

Got through our day[']s travel and camped close by Ft. Bridger. A very pretty place and best of all plenty of grass, and wild rye for the horses. A great abundance of clear pretty water by a small creek.

Thursday 11th [August]

A beautiful morning, quite cool, laid over to-day to rest and recruit our horses a little. We wrote to Mary Ann to-day, wrote six sheets of letter paper. I think that will do her till we get to Salt Lake.

Friday 12th [August]

Another pleasant morning but rather cool, pretty near ready to leave camp

Started [on.] Went to Ft. Bridger, about a mile from where we camped, put a letter in the office for Mary Ann[,] left there about nine o'clock. The Dr. was told not to go the telegraph road[,] but to take the Mormon road to Salt Lake. The telegraph road the grass was all about all eat off, most of the travel being along there, the Mormon road we would find plenty of feed and pretty good roads.

We took their advice and found plenty of good feed. A large rich Valley of splendid grass. We came over some mountainous country to-day, looked quite Romantic in some parts. Had a very pretty view of the Wasach Mountains this morning[,] covered with snow[.] It looks very pretty.

Crossed Big Muddy. We have camped at a very nice place close by some Springs, having come 19 miles to-day.

Saturday 13th [August]

A clear pretty morning, very cold. Started from camp about 6 o'clock. Crossed over some mountains and tolerable rough rocky roads. It appeared a long day's ride although not going not more than eighteen miles.

We are now camped by a creek about four miles from Bear River, it is rather a pretty place to camp.

Just before we had fixed on the right camping place[,] we saw an indian laying on the ground between some bushes watching us. The Dr. went and talked with him, found out that he was one of the Snake Indians, the Siouxs had been fighting. He is what is called a friendly Indian. He tried to get us to understand the

Siouxs had killed some of his papooses and taken all they had from them, they running away from them barely saved their lives.

He appeared to be watchful and very uneasy. After a little[,] his squaw and one child came and stayed till dark. We gave them some bread and meat.

About a hundred miles back I should think[,] there was 25 Sioux indians seen in the night on their returning from the fight with the Snakes, they carried along many scalps, and maybe this poor indian's children was some of them.

Sunday 14th [August]

A cold morning, soon be ready to leave camp, intend going as far as Bear River where we intend laying over a few days[.]

Went 4 miles to day. Mattie washed to-day. Lizzie did the cooking.

Monday 15th [August]

Came 4 miles to Bear Creek Sunday morning, laid over, intend starting this morning, a pretty clear morning.

Bear River is a nice stream, the water clear and pure. Started from the river about nine this morning, came over some rocky hilly, mountainous roads. Saw some high massive looking rock, I should think some three or four hundred feet high, one of the rocks back a little had the appearance of a wigwam, but looking through the Marine Glass we discovered it to be a rock. It was one of nature's great curiosity and wonderful work. The scenery is picturesque and grand in a great many parts. We had some beautiful landscape views to-day.

We at last crossed Chalk Creek, went a mile or two farther, came to a Mormon Rancho, where we camped close by the river. We are told when we go ten miles farther we will find it difficult to get grass for our horses, so many going through it is all eat up. Oats $5.00 a bushel and every thing else high in proportion. We are 50 miles from Salt Lake. I shall be glad. We traveled to-day 22 miles.

The 1864 Diary of Mrs. Sarah Jane Rousseau

Tuesday 16th [August]

Last night got in a different atmosphere, having descended some fifteen hundred feet down the mountains. It makes a great difference in our feelings, being so much warmer and pleasant, almost ready to make another start this morning[.] It is cloudy looks some like rain.

Left camp[,] went about 2 miles[,] crossed over one very bad hill and crossed the creek. Camped in a Valley by Chalk Creek with mountains on either side of us.

Wednesday 17th [August]

Rained some last night, this morning bright and clear. Mrs. Day's family and two others left this morning for Salt Lake. Also Newton Honeywell left.

Thursday 18th [August]

A bright clear pleasant morning, but quite cold, intend going seven miles this morning to a Mormon blacksmith to have the tires of our waggon made smaller and some horseshoeing done. We expect our train to come up with us there.

Got to the Mormon settlement, it is quite a village, a number of houses, some look neat and clean. They are most all made with small round logs, some have made the roof tolerable high and sloping, covered with shingles but most of the houses are very low and covered with dirt.

One of the Mormons let us camp in their enclosure[.] After we stopped[,] a Mormon woman came to the carriage, asked if Mattie was sick. I told her she was not very well. She said they had a first rate doctor with them. I told her my husband was a doctor. She then told me she was a poor woman, that her husband died in the spring and how poor her health was, that she would like to have a talk with me if I was alone.

I got out of the carriage and went with her at the back of the waggon in the shade, had quite a conversation with her about her disease both of body and mind[.] She appeared a good deal afflicted and wanted me to ask the Dr. one question[,] which I did. She then said the doctors differed a good deal in their opinions, and she was a greater curiosity than ever, gave me an invitation to go to her house. I told [her] I could not walk that far. She then bid me goodbye.

The road we came over to-day was rough and hilly. Some of the settlers said they had a hard rain a few weeks ago, and they supposed a cloud had burst over the mountains where we passed along. It must have been an awful rain[,] the immense quantity of stones that were washed from the mountains small and large, some weighing I should think tons. We suppose it must have been a waterspout that opened up its great waters. And[,] from the appearance of the Canyon[,] there must have been a great flood of waters.

We are camped in a pretty Valley on the Weber River, about as large as stream as Bear River[.]

Came 7 miles to-day.

Friday 19th [August]

Another pleasant morning. A warm gentle wind stirring. Got our blacksmithing done, are waiting for our train to come along when we might well make another start.

The Mormons appear to be an industrious people, they have made considerable improvements, have tolerable large fields of oats, wheat and some corn. It looked so pretty to see such things growing once again, it made me feel good to think we were in reach of civilization once more. I wish we were at the end of our long journey.

We still keep hearing of the great depredations and mischief the Indians are committing[.] Where we passed along from Ft. Kearney and Laramie they have destroyed some trains by burning the waggons and murdering the emigrants. I don't know how true it is, but if the statements are true I hope there is a great deal of exaggeration about it.

We saw our train across [*word missing*.] The Dr. went to see them and have some talk[.]

He has returned, said they had gone on but did not know how far they were going this evening, gave no particular satisfaction about their movements.

Saturday 20th [August]

A white frost this morning, but now it is warm and pleasant. While here we bought eight quarts of milk and one pound of butter which we paid one dollar and seventy-five cents, then a dollar and half for pasturage for horses and 1/2 dollar for something. Soon ready to leave camp[.]

Started about half past eight, went through a Kanyon to-day seven miles long, it appeared to me both tedious and dangerous the road good part of the way on the mountain side (mountains on both side of the Creek) to look down from the road to Silver Creek which runs through the Kanyon[.] Made me feel afraid if the horses had taken fright at anything, the road being so narrow[,] we might have been turned over and dashed to pieces. I felt more afraid traveling along that mountain side than any part of the journey.

We came up with our train this evening. We are camped at a ranch on silver Creek, rather a pretty place[.]

Came 15 miles to-day.

Sunday 21st [August]

Last evening it clouded up looked a good deal like rain, the wind raised and it blew hard most of the night. I was afraid it would blow the waggon over.

Started from camp at half past eight this morning. The road most of the way rough and hilly, went several miles through a Kanyon, nooned by a spring of good cold water, crossed over what is called the summit, about 18 or 20 miles distant from Salt Lake City[.]

We are now camped close by a creek almost surrounded by mountains about thirteen miles from the Great City[.]

To-day is John's birthday, 12 years old[.]

Made 14 miles to-day.

Monday 22nd [August]

A very rainy disagreeable morning.

Started from camp about 7 o'clock, camped in the Kanyon last night. Went mile after mile, it seems as though we would never get there going over the mountains up hill[,] down hill, rocks and uneven roads, at last over a very high mountain. The last one about 3 or 4 miles from the City.

After so long a time we arrived at the great Salt Lake City. The Salt Lake Valley which has been so highly eulogised for the fertility of its soil, its productiveness, I was greatly disappointed in[.] They must have considerable trouble [with] what they raise [because] they have to irrigate[.] There is a certainty then of crops[.] Instead of seeing the Valley covered with luxurious grass[,] nothing but wild sage, and sandy soil.

The city did not come up the least to my expectations. The houses are mostly low adobe buildings, as many houses in the enclosure as the man has wives[.] some real miserable looking places to live in[.] I suppose according to the estimate he places on the different women so he has the houses fixed. Yet there are some pretty looking buildings.

I understand there is plenty of people that are not Mormons living here, and likely they don't build the same way. They appear to have a taste for trees, there is a good many through the city.

Yesterday morning[,] I understand[,] the mountains around the City were covered with snow. Mattie has gone to the city to see if she can get a situation as a teacher for the winter[,] as we are uncertain where [she] will go. We want to stay a few weeks to recruit our horses.

(This morning we got a sight of the city[.] Was very unfavorable, raining and very foggy. We could not see any distance. I was real sorry it was not a clear pretty day. I wanted to have a good view of it. Those that could go round and look at the city say there are some very handsome buildings.)

(Was very much disappointed did not get getting some letters at Salt Lake.)

Tuesday 23rd [August]

Mattie has returned and came to the conclusion while in Salt Lake [*words missing*.]

It has been quite showery all day. I looked through the marine glass a while ago at the snow on the mountains that fell yesterday, it looked very pretty. The mountains around the City are above the clouds[,] a good many of them.

Wednesday 24th [August]

Rained most all night, looks something like clearing off this morning, we think of leaving the Great City.

It is rumored here there has been two Mormon trains destroyed by the indians and the people all massacred. A false report, had trouble with the indians but got through safe.

Mattie changed her mind this evening, thought it best to go along with us.

Went 5 or 6 miles and camped with our train. Where we camped until next morning and had plenty of feed for the horses, and bought half bushel of potatoes at 4 dollars per bushel.

Just as we were ready and started[,] Mattie took another notion, and said she thought she better stay at Salt Lake, she did not feel well enough to travel any farther. I told her she knew best, she was plenty old enough to judge for herself. I talked to her as if she were my own daughter. When she wanted to stay at Salt Lake and teach school through the winter without a female acquaintance or any person she knew[,] I told her I thought it an important step for her to take.

She finally said she would rather go on with us, if it would not cost her too much. I told her if that was her reason for staying in the city[,] she need not let that cause her any uneasiness. I had not thought anything about it and I did not expect the Dr. had. Well[,] she had a talk with the Dr. that amounted to pretty much the same she had with me. He told her whatever she owed him when we got through, she might pay him when she could and if she could not pay him anything he did not care, that need not be the means of her staying back.

I don't know what to make of her, she has changed her mind so many times, and told different tales, told me she did not feel able to go any farther, she did not feel well enough, told the Dr. she would rather go with us, if she would be able to pay the expensive going.

After we started[,] she changed again and said she believed she would stay back, had her things taken out of the waggon and we left as she appeared determined to stay.

Went a few miles and was told mattie was in the waggon behind with Tom Hays and his wife. I felt some surprise yet not a great deal as she had changed her mind so often.

Traveled about 20 miles, it was quite dark when we got to the camping place, no water or grass[.] Went to bed without getting any supper only eating a little bread that we had baked, and boiled a few ears of corn.

Friday 26th [August]

A pleasant morning, very warm.

Started from camp as soon as we geared up without our breakfast[.] Thought by going a few miles we would get some feed for our horses[.] Went about 5 miles to Utah Lake[,] a pretty smooth body of water. There was a farm close by, got the horses in a pasture and eat our own breakfast[.]

There was a spring of hot water close to the house. I was rolled in the carriage to see it. I got out and put my hands in it, it appeared pretty near boiling hot, the people of the house said it was hard water, they couldn't wash with it, if it could have been used for washing clothes I should have thought a very valuable spring.

We are now about ready to make another start, went a few miles[,] met Richard Curtis coming for us. Said Em. was very sick[.] The Dr. said she had what is called mountain fever.

Got to the camping pretty close to the Lake, found plenty of grass and water, quite a pretty situation to camp, but I think it sickly having being inundated recently and now drying out. The masma that is continually rising and unpleasant sulfurous smell gives strong indication of a sickly place.

We thought of leaving this morning and go to a more healthy situation, but Mrs. Hays was taken sick about midnight. Mr. Curtis came and awoke us[,] the Dr. to go and see her. I suppose we shall remain on her account.

Made it about 15 miles to-day.

Saturday 27th [August]

The Dr. was up all night attending to Mrs. H.[,] Em Curtis appears some better this morning.

We are traveling on the West side of the Lake, being told we would find better grass on that side. Mrs. Hays had a find son about 10 o'clock Saturday night[,] August 27th. Em Curtis still sick.

Sunday 28th [August]

A very pleasant morning. I walked over to see Mrs. Hays this morning with the help of Elizabeth. Mrs. Hays is quite smart. I stayed with her about an hour and then went to see Em Curtis. I found her some little better. I then went to see Mrs. Hamilton a while and returned home.

We think of starting from this sickly place if Mrs. H and Em Curtis are able to travel.

Mr. Earp and family left this morning to get to a more healthy situation[,] several of the family being sick.

Monday 29th [August]

Quite a pleasant morning. Mrs. Hays quite smart to-day. Em Curtis some better. The grey mare that has been sick with the colic, we did not expect she would get over it, but she is some better now, she looks dreadfully bad.
I hope we will be able to leave this sickly place before long[.] The weather is exceedingly warm.

Tuesday 30th [August]

Another warm morning. Clear and pleasant. I thought likely we would be able to move from the sickly place to-day. Think it running too great a risk to move Em Curtis yet, although she is improving slowly. Mrs. Hays is doing well.

There was quite a wind started a while ago, it is now raining pretty smart showers, feels a good deal cooler than it has been for some little time back.

Wednesday 31st [August]

This morning real pleasant, nice breeze stirring. Cannot leave camp yet. We think Em Curtis cannot be moved yet with safety.

It has been quite showery all day.

Mr. Parker left us to-day. He has not felt well for several days, thought he needed rest. He went back to Salt Lake. I hope we won't be detained here any length of time period I think it quite a sickly place.

Oh how I wish we were at the end of our long journey[.] If the Indians are not troublesome, it will not be many weeks e're we will be at the end of our route.

(Detained here a week on account of Mr. Curtis's family. Em [too] sick with the mountain fever and Mrs. Hays encouchment.)

Thursday 1st [September]

Quite a cool pleasant morning the wind blew hard all night and is still blowing pretty smart breeze.

Em Curtis is doing well. I hope we will be able to proceed on our journey before long. Went to see Em Curtis this afternoon[.] She seems to be improving slowly.

Went to see Mrs. Hamilton for a while, both her and the baby are well. Mrs. Hays is doing well. Mattie Field is working for them. She talks something of going back to Salt Lake.

Friday 2nd [September]

A cool pleasant morning[.] Blew hard all night, still blowing a smart breeze[.]

The sick are some better. We think of making a move this morning to some healthy situation. We were told there was good feed five miles from this place and a more healthy place to camp.

Geared up and made a start, went I think fully 6 miles and came to a pretty good Adobe house with three tolerable sized rooms below and one above, shingled roof and fire place in each room[.] They said the occupants had left it about three weeks, when we took possession of it right away.

It is the first time I have been in a house since I left home, it really felt good to be in a house once again. I think if I ever end the happy owner of a home again I shall know how to appreciate its comforts. And another blessing I shall know how to appreciate, that of walking. I walked alone when I got in the house.

Oh how proud I felt, I suppose I felt the pride and happiness of a little child when it finds out it can walk alone. Those can realize the great privilege but those that have to forgo the comfort and blessing of walking. I hardly know how to express the satisfaction and thankfulness I feel to our Heavenly Father for all his tender mercies towards me. May I ever praise his Great and Holy name.

Saturday 3rd [September]

Quite cool and pleasant morning, nothing disturbed our repose last night. The wind blew hard all night. A good many of the company slept in the Adobe house. I slept in the carriage.

The sick ones are convalescent this morning. We think of making another start this morning and go about 15 miles.

Started from our Adobe habitation about 8 o'clock. A few minutes before starting[,] Mr. White came in a waggon for Mattie Field, from

Salt Lake. Mattie went back with Mr. W. She is a strange girl. I don't know what to make of her. I hope she may do well.

We started on our way and went as far as Goshen at the end of Lake Utah, having passed by Mount Nebo, a high mountain on the West side of L.U. The mountains look grand. I think from the appearance the West side of the Lake, it would be a pleasant place to live. Goshen is a small Mormon settlement.

We are still in danger of the Indians. We saw two this morning. We were told there were three horses stolen last night, two not far from where we started and one from Goshen.

Went 15 miles to-day[.] Bought some oats for our horses. Poor things they look awful. I feel so sorry for them.

Sunday 4th [September]

A cool and pleasant morning, the sick are all better, intend going about 10 miles where Mr. Earp is camping. We heard there was good grass and water there[.] If there is[,] we intend to lay over a while.

Before leaving the place Goshen[,] the Dr. was called in to see a sick boy[.] They thought he had the mountain fever, thought he could not live, but they happened to hear by some man how sick Em Curtis had been and was getting well, and they would have the Dr. go and see if he could do anything for them. He went to see him[,] found out he was a very sick boy, gave him some medicine and left directions how to take it, and for them to come the next day where we were camped and let him know how he was.

While the Dr. was gone to see the boy[,] a Mormon woman came to the waggon where I was and asked me if I had any dried fruit or sugar to trade her. I told her I hadn't any to spare as we had to buy at Salt Lake while we were there. She staid at the carriage a good while talking with me, invited me to go and see her and finally said she would like to have us stop there.

The Mormons seem to be very friendly disposed people[.] In Goshen they are most of them from England. I heard while there[,] a family by the name of Leonard, that I was acquainted with in Burlington[.] He was a blind man[.] They told me she was living at Salt Lake, that him and her were not living together. She by some means had got all the property in her hands and he was in California[,] that he occasionally came to see her. I suppose she is a Mormon. If I had heard about her while we were at Salt Lake, I would have liked to have gone to see her.

We started from Goshen and went through Salt Creek Kanyon and came in Juab Valley, Juab County[.] It is a very pretty Valley[.] There is a settlement called Clover Creek where there is a P.O. called Mona Post Office, 4 miles from where we have camped.

We found Mr. Earp. Since he left us[,] one of our mares he was using took sick with the same complaint our gray mare had, the colic, and died[.] It is quite a loss for us. I think it likely if he had stayed where we were[,] the Dr. would have cured her[.]

Came about ten miles to-day.

Monday 5th [September]

Quite cool this morning. Elizabeth washed to-day. The sick folks are convalescent. We think of moving close to the mountains, there is better water and grass to be got. It won't be near as much trouble for us to move our camping place as taking our horses there to feed every time, besides the [missing word] is so much more handy[.] Where we are is nothing but sage to burn. We don't know whether any of our company will go with us or not.

A boy came from Goshen this morning to let us know the boy that was sick was better and wanted more medicine for him. Sent him some with directions how to use it and let us know next day if he were better.

Tuesday 6th [September]

Another cool morning[.] The sick are all still improving. Geared up and went close to the mountain camp. We are close to Mount Nebo[,] a much nicer and more pleasant place, plenty of pure good water, grass and wood, and great deal cleaner place to camp, the rest of the company have not come yet.

Elizabeth is ironing some to-day. I thought we had passed by Mount Nebo but was mistaken. We are close by it now. There is a settlement twelve miles South of here called Nephi[,] which we will pass through when we leave.

Wednesday 7th [September]

A pleasant morning, nothing disturbed our repose last night. The Dr., Messrs. Curtis, Hamilton, Hays went up the Kanyon to hunt bear, but returned without any[.]

Haven't heard anything about the sick boy at Goshen, think it likely he is dead.

Thursday 8th [September]

Blowed dreadful hard all night, the wind abated before we got up. It is a warm wind and blowing a pretty soft breeze since the sun arose.

Elizabeth, John and Albert went down to the other camp a while ago. Libby has got back and said some of them are talking of coming here to camp a while. I wish they would[.] it is rather lonesome to be by ourselves. The boy stayed a while longer than Libby but have returned back and said some of them had moved to another camping place, some are in favor of coming where we are and some don't want to.

They killed a beef down there to-day. The Dr. went this evening to get some of it. They have very good beef and mutton here.

Libby is expecting Eliza Curtis and Jane Hamilton to visit her to-day. It is two miles and a half from their camping place to where we are.

Friday 9th [September]

The wind went down last night. Nothing disturbed us[.] This morning is very pleasant, bright and clear, our horses seem to be improving a little, they appeared a good deal more lively.

Libby's company did not come to-day. The Dr. went on the mountain to-day to take a survey of the surrounding country, he came back tired out, looked real sick, he said it took him five hours to climb the mountain, it is a chain of the Wasatch Mountains. He said when he got to the top he looked at Mount Nebo which appeared to him as much higher to the top of it as the Wasatch does to us in the Valley below. There is one continuous range of mountains on each side of us, one towering above the other. They have a very beautiful and imposing appearance.

It is Picturesque, Grand, but to the weary traveler who is over anxious to get to their journey[`]s end and in continual danger of hostile Indians, and if not hostile, but what they termed peaceable indians, they are around at all anytime stealing horses, which keeps a person continually uneasy and on the watch for fear their stock will be stolen from them.

A way back about Fort Kearney and Laramie, the Indians would make a dash in the daytime and take your horses[.] Here it is different, they come skulking in the night to steal. If [only] there was no danger of Indians and the company all sociable, but it seems to me they appear to be offish from what reason I cannot tell. Our journey has been mixed with a great deal of unpleasantness.

Saturday 10th [September]

Another pleasant morning, looking through the Marine glass a while ago[,] we discovered our company leaving. They never intimated their intention although they came for their horses last night that were grazing close to where we were camped. The first of our knowing anything of their moving was in looking through the Marine glass and seen them all move away but one waggon[,] which was coming toward our camp.

The Dr. went to meet that waggon to find out their intentions. He went on horseback and said if Mr. Earp was going to act the rascal about going off with our property that he would go to the next town and get a writ and try to get our property in our own hands again.

Oh how bad I feel this morning, considering our situation. Myself and three children left here alone in suspense until the Dr. gets back to let us know what they intend doing.

He met Mr. Curtis coming to our camp to have his boy attended to, he thought he was taking the same fever Em had, the rest of the company having gone on. The Dr. told him he would like to know what they intend doing, as they hadn't sent any word [that] they intended leaving. Mr. Curtis said they intended to go and get better grass for their horses, if they couldn't find it, as their horses wasn't improving much.

Now we could see that our horses were improving materially on the grass where we were, but for some cause they didn't come there. Mr. Curtis said he told Dick this morning before when he came up after the horses, they being at our camping place, to let us know they were going to leave, but he didn't do it.

The 1864 Diary of Mrs. Sarah Jane Rousseau

Mr. Curtis wanted the Dr. to prescribe for his boy. The Dr. told him he had no medicine with him, couldn't do anything for him there and he wanted to know where Mr. Earp was going.

That Mr. Earp had acted strange, he had left once before. We having to stay on account of Em Curtis and Mrs. Hays being sick. After he left us[,] one of our mares that he was using took sick and died, and when we saw him he never so much as hinted anything about her to him. We think he acted very curious to say the least of it. He must know we feel some little interest in our property and think as a friend he ought to say something to us about her[.] Ttis a good deal of a loss to us.

Sunday 11th [September]

Quite a stormy night the wind blowing hard and raining, this morning the wind still blowing and showery[.] Iit looks very curious to see the clouds come below the high mountains[.] It appears like clouds of smoke. They completely hide the top of Mount Nebo, but that is such a very high one period it is 12,000 feet above the level of the sea.

A range of the Wasatch Mountains above where we camped appear very high, the clouds come considerable below the top of them, but Mount Nebo is as high again as they are.

We geared up and made another start[.] Passed by Mona settlement, went through the town of Nephi, the County seat of Juab. Nephi is a good sized town, and some nice Adobe buildings and quite a good looking church. I think they will have a pretty town after a while. There was a number of new buildings going up[.]

Went a few miles farther and stopped for the night, there was plenty of good grass but neither wood or water handy, we happened to fill two small kegs with water at our last camping place, which furnished our supper and breakfast and got sagewood to cook with[.] We traveled about sixteen miles to-day.

Monday 12th [September]

Had a comfortable night's rest[,] nothing disturbed us. A bright clear morning, the wind rising and quite cool, making ready for another start[.] Our poor horses need water badly. Got where there was water which the horses partook of bountifully[.]

Went on[.] Passed through Chicken Creek settlement, a small place and not very pretty. Here we heard of our company. They camped here last night. They started on this morning intended going as far as Seiver River to lay over a while. We think of going as far as Chicken Creek after dinner.

Went on over Chicken Creek[,] found no grass, and went as far as Siever River, taking us till ten o'clock to get there, it was a pretty moonlit night, found some high coarse grass for the horses to eat, thought it better than nothing, did not find our company there, they had gone on farther about 20 miles.

Tuesday 13th [September]

A cold morning, froze hard last night, rather cold preparing breakfast out doors, think of starting as soon as we eat breakfast and harness up.

Seiver R. is quite [a] narrow stream and muddy, there was a good bridge across it. It was a very unpleasant camping place[.]

Started from camp rather late[,] having the harness to fix different to be easier on the poor horses, they appear to be very much tuckered out. It was a quarter past eleven when we got started, went a short distance to a Canyon, met with a Mormon that had been camping there all night, had his horses close by on the mountain eating bunch grass, which is the best feed for them, they will get fat on it in a short time. His name is G. Huntsman.

The Dr. and him had a long talk, the Mormons appear real friendly people. We bought a dollars worth of Peaches of him at fifty cents per dozen[.] He had some pickled cucumbers a small keg, which he asked ten dollars for. We did not buy it, thought it was too much. I should like to have had them first rate.

He gave us some directions telling us the best roads to go, told us to get to round Valley settlement where there was a Post Office. I had written a letter to Mary Ann to send out the first opportunity, so I put it in the Office there. The Dr. said they told him the mail went through on the Plains again, the Indians had quit their depredations.

We went through the settlement into a Canyon where we camped for the night. There was a family come up to the Canyon after we did and camped a little below us.

After a while another waggon came along and passed by us, and then another[.] The man came to us and stayed awhile then his wife got out of the waggon to warm herself. We had a good fire. It was a very cold night. They were Mormons on their way home. I suppose they had been visiting. They live in Dixie about 200 miles from this place. They advised us to go there to live.

This man's name was Dayton, he told us he was going through to Southern California in about two months from now in a Mormon train. The Dr. said we would like to go along with him, it is much safer traveling along with them on account of the Indians, they don't trouble them any.

We intend laying over to rest our horses[,] it will take pretty near that time for them to get fat and go the 200 miles[.] He wanted us to call and see them. I think it likely we shall and maybe go through with their train yet this fall.

Wednesday 14th [September]

A very cold morning, got ready to leave camp as soon as possible[.] Went seven miles to wild goose springs where we were advised and lay over there being plenty of good grass, wood and water.

Got to the Springs about three o'clock[,] found a very good camping place where we intend staying a few days. We found the rest of our train, they had got there at the day before. Our horses are now resting and having plenty of good feed.

Thursday 15th [September]

A pleasant morning good deal warmer than it has been a few days back.

Mr. Earp left this morning. The rest of the train intend laying over a few days.

Mrs. Curtis and Hamilton came up this morning to see us. They intend moving their camping place. They don't like it where they are.

We are surrounded by mountains. There is considerable timber mostly low cedar trees and oak. Considerable [amounts] of wild sage around.

An Indian just rode up on his pony[,] had his gun[,] bow and arrow[.] He looked like a Chief. We did not understand each other very well. He did not stay long. I don't like to see any of them.

(Wild Goose Springs[,] 140 miles South of Great Salt Lake City, Millard County U.T. 1864.)

Friday 16th [September]

Last night was pretty[,] bright moonlight[.] The girls Jane Hamilton and Eliza Curtis came and stayed with Libby all night.

This morning is warm and pleasant, a nice breeze stirring. Libby intends washing to-day. I have had a day of mending the boys clothes.

A good many wild cattle came up pretty close to our camp. We tried to drive them off but they looked pretty saucy[,] stood staring at us, then Dr. fired five shots of his revolver at them, they all skedadled in a hurry. I feel afraid of them. They came up when Libby and I was alone. I felt real frightened. I did not know what they might do, so I yelled at them as loud as I could, they looked at us real impudent. I kept hollering at them till I scared them, they all ran off in pretty fast trot[.]

Libby said I was enough to scare anything with the noise I made. I was very glad I could frighten them at all, we heard their owners dare not go among them without a revolver or a gun.

The rest of the company have moved their camping place about a quarter of a mile farther from us. They sent word for us to go and camp with them. I think likely we would have gone if the water where they have gone had been clear and nice, but it is too nasty for us to use, the cattle and horses making it so filthy.

Where we are we have pure clean spring water, nothing can get to it. The Dr. cleaned it all out all nice[,] walled it up and covered it over with a rock. We have abundance good grass for the horses, and plenty of wood[.]

Thought it better to stay where we are. The boys and their Pa went out to see if they could kill a Jack rabbit. They got one and brought it for our breakfast.

They went down to the other camp[.] It was a good while after sundown when they got back, Libby and I felt pretty lonesome before they returned.

Saturday 17th [September]

A cloudy morning has every appearance of rain. It has cleared off nice and warm. Cooked the rabbit for breakfast. It was very nice eating. It is the first one we have tasted. I think they are nicer than the ones we have at home.

From where we are camped we can see plain Savier Lake, twenty five miles long and ten miles wide about 20 miles West of us. It has a pretty appearance[.]

We think of remaining where we are till Monday. With no preventing Providence[,] we will make another start on our journey.

Sunday 18th [September]

Last evening thundered and rained. Since cleared off cool and pleasant, had a beautiful moonlight night.

The Kiotes came close to our camp and eat some bones and meat Libby had thrown out. We heard the barking when we got up.

This is a warm clear morning, been very pleasant all day. Had the prettiest sunset I most ever saw. The clouds appeared fringed with gold after a little the brightness disappeared and in place of it clouds of a deep rose color, it was indeed beautiful to look at.

Monday 19th [September]

A pleasant morning. Intend starting from camp as soon as we get ready. Started about ten o'clock[,] came through Cedar Springs settlement, a small place.

Went on to Fillmore, a real nice town, some good looking Adobe houses with Peach Orchards close by them. (Traveled 11 miles.)

Tuesday 20th [September]

We had our satisfaction of nice ripe peaches while we stopped[,] which was pretty near all day.

A good many in the train were busy trading. (Made about 15 miles to-day.)

Wednesday 21st [September]

Started from camp about 9 o'clock. A warm pleasant morning. It was late when we got to a camping place last night. Very little grass and no water, came about three miles to Corn Creek where we met with Mr. Earp, he was waiting there for us.

[**Note in margin reads:** The name of this place is Petersburg, commonly called the Corn Creek settlement.]

The rest of our company stayed back where we were camped[,] having lost some of their cattle. Could not see them anywhere[,] thought the Indians had run them off. We had to leave them on account of our horses having nothing to eat.

There are plenty of the natives about us, all sizes, sex and ages.

The rest of the company came on in the afternoon but had not found their cattle.

Thursday 22nd [September]

A cool cloudy morning. The Dr. and the rest of the company this morning made arrangements with the Indian Chief Canuse to take care of our horses for a month, which he promised to do, taking all the responsibility of them, paying him a dollar per head for attending them. Tom Hays and Dick Curtis with an indian went this morning to hunt their cattle, the indian said he knew where they were, but they returned without them, couldn't find them. The indians will hunt for them I think.

Last night one of the elders, Orson Hyde, one of the twelve apostles[,] I suppose[,] came and had a long talk with the company, stayed until a late hour[.] He seemed quite communitive. It seems a characteristic among the Mormons to be kind and talkative[.] They all appear anxious to have immigrants settle among them.

The settlers are expecting the president Brigham Young with all his train to stop here tonight on his return from Dixie to Great Salt Lake City. I suppose we shall have the pleasure of seeing his Highness. They suppose we will have a ball. He is very fond of encouraging all such amusements. It is said he is very pleasant and affable to every class of people. The people all speak well of him.

Friday 23rd [September]

A pleasant bright morning, expected Brigham Young with his escort last evening. They didn't come till this morning. There was a number of waggons in several carriages.

The President[,] as the people call him[,] was in a four horse carriage. He touched his hat and bowed very politely to me as they passed by. His wife was with him. The Mormon said he was going to preach to them tonight.
I did not have a very good look at the President, could only see him as they passed by in a closed carriage, he appeared to be a good looking fleshy gentleman. I would like to have been a little nearer to him to have had a good look at him. They put up at a house about a half mile from where we are camped.

A Mormon insisted the Dr., Messrs. Curtis, Hamilton and Earp with some others to go down and see Brigham Young. They went and had an introduction, conversed with him about an hour. They said he was easy in his manners, affable and a good deal of a gentleman. Was somewhat reserved, appeared tired, having traveled 48 miles to-day.

Didn't have preaching as was supposed, on account of having traveled so far they were tired out. The musicians played some few times on the brass band then all was still.

Saturday 24th [September]

Was aroused this morning by [a] Band playing some very pretty tunes. It was just about the break of day when they commenced having their arrangements[.] Made to breakfast at Fillmore[,] a distance of 12 miles from here. So that was the last of Brigham Young and his Haram.

[**Margin notation reads**: The music sounded delightful when all was still. One tune they played, a great favorite of mine ["]A Life on the Ocean Wave["] with two others that I was acquainted with. How reviving to my feelings in the still hour, Break of Day.]

After a while we got up. A pretty clear warm morning. After breakfast Libby washed the clothes. I hardly know how to make myself contented till the horses are recruited sufficiently to get through our long and dangerous journey. I suppose we will have to remain about six weeks before they will be able to go.

Sunday 25th [September]

A cloudy morning sprinkled a few drops of rain. As it hardly rains here I suppose it will soon clear off.

The Dr. and Mr. Earp have gone to see about the horses. They can't be seen anywhere. We feel afraid all the time some of the indians will run them off. Oh how I wish we were where we would never see another indian.

Mr. Curtis was reading the newspaper to a number of them in the tent last night where he saw the trial of Mr. White in the abduction of Miss Field. We don't believe the charge she has alleged against Mr. White[,] only knew some of the [story.] he said Miss Field had written a letter to Mr. White but didn't know what she had written. That Mr. White came with the waggon to Utah Lake on the morning we were ready to start on with the intention of taking Miss F. back with him to Salt Lake.

She said he had come after her. We went on and left her at Utah Lake to go back with him to Salt Lake. She went with him voluntarily.

I should like to have the papers with the trial. I want to know all about it. We felt very much surprised to see such announcement in the papers[,] not having heard anything about her since we left it her at U. Lake. She had left us about two weeks [ago] and was traveling with Tom Hays and wife. Consequently[,] we knew nothing about her arrangements[,] only what we heard others say.

It has been cloudy and windy all day sprinkled a little rain.

Monday 26th [September]

Blowed hard all night. This morning, warm and pleasant. Found all the horses last night.

It has been pretty pleasant all day, but rather windy, towards night it clouded up and rained some.

[**On the back of the first page of the diary, the following statement is found**: "The Dr. sent the sewing machine, carpet and some books with a Mormon train going to California, San Bernardino. The Mormons name is Guard."]

Tuesday 27th [September]

Had quite a stormy night[.] The wind blew very hard, it thundered, lightnened, hailed and rained. This morning it is clear and serene.

Yesterday[,] the Dr. sent the sewing machine, carpets and some books in a Mormon freight train to San Bernardino, California.

I visited Mrs. Curtis to-day, took dinner with them, came back and stayed a while with Mrs. Earp, came home and went to bed.

Wednesday 28th [September]

This morning very pleasant rather cool. It blew some during the night. After sun up a while[,] it was warm and pleasant.
Canuse (pronounced Kanoss), the Indian Chief, took breakfast with us.

Thursday 29th [September]

I went over to see Mrs. Hamilton[,] stayed until after dinner.

Called on Mrs. Jesse Curtis, had some chit chat[,] after which Mrs. Curtis and I went to Mrs. Hamilton's. I then came home.

The Dr.[,] Mr. Earp and Mr. Hatten went to Fillmore this morning, did not get back till after dark, brought us some Peaches. The Dr. brought us bushel and half, the others bought some for their wives.

Friday 30th [September]

A beautiful morning. Canuse took breakfast in the tent this morning[.] After we had done eating, the Dr. has gone to hunt Albert's Philly, she was missing yesterday.

The indians look awful to-day, so many of them. Their faces painted all over[,] different colors. Six or seven of them have just been round the waggon all painted up[,] talking to me. They are enough to frighten anybody, they look so savage. I wish we were where we would never see another. They pester us all day, begging every thing they see.

October Saturday 1st

This morning cold and clear[.] after sun up[,] it was warm and pleasant, not quite so windy as it has been, last night it blew up cold.

The Dr. and I wrote to Mary Ann and sent it by Mr. Robinson as all the mail was to leave early this morning.

Sunday 2nd [October]

This morning is very pleasant, rather cool but I think it will be warm after a while.

Last night a Mormon woman by the name of Hibbert came to see me. In the course of our conversation she spoke of having lived in Newcastle on Tyne, I immediately asked her if she was acquainted with a man by the name of Thomas Elliot, a Preacher, and kept a large boot and shoe establishment. She said she was, had seen him[,] and said he was a large fleshy man.

I told her he was my Uncle, Mother's brother. She appeared astonished as much as I was, meeting with a person in Utah Territory, and she a Mormon to be acquainted with my Uncle. I began to think we needn't feel surprised at anything in these days.

I went to see Mrs. Hatten to-day. She was sick with the chills and fever. They intend going south with us. I think they will be ready to go in two weeks.

This has been a cold windy day.

Monday 3rd [October]

This morning cold. There was a thick cake of ice on the bucket of water.

Now it is warm and pleasant. Elizabeth is washing to-day.

Tuesday 4th [October]

Pleasant morning but rather cool, bids fair to be a pleasant day. Kanoss, the Indian Chief took breakfast with us this morning.

Mr. Hatten and his family are making preparations to go with us in about two weeks to Southern California. They are Mormons from the old country. They appear to be a very friendly people.

Wednesday 5th [October]

A warm pleasant morning. Kanoss took breakfast with us again.

One of the oxen Mr. Earp had was seen this morning with an arrow shot in his shoulder. Mr. Earp came pretty near getting us all in trouble with his temper, swearing and cutting up. The Chief got dreadfully mad at him and swore at him. I was very much afraid they would get mad at us.

Mr. Hatten was close by an indian that could talk indian. He tried to explain to Kanoss, and get Earp him to shake hands. Kanoss would not at first, but put his hands behind him, and seemed dreadfully mad.

The Indians kept coming until there was near a dozen, there appeared to be a great danger of having a fuss with them. But Mr. Hatten at last got Kanoss and Earp to shake hands, and I hope that will be the last of it.

Thursday 6th [October]

A warm clear and pleasant morning. The Dr. & Mr. & Mrs. Hatten went to Fillmore this morning. Went to Mill, don't expect them back till morning.

Mr. Parker came to-day. I expect he intends to go with us to Southern California.

Friday 7th [October]

Last night was very pleasant. This morning warm and smoky, looks like the Indian Summer has commenced.

Oh how ardently I wish we were at the end of our journey. I suppose we will leave this place in about a week's time, to try our luck across the desert. I hope we will get safe through, but I am very much afraid of the Indians. They appear inclined to be pretty saucy even in this place.

Saturday 8th [October]

A warm pleasant morning. I went to see Mrs. Hatten to-day, she was sick in bed. I stayed with her pretty much all day. She felt better this evening.

Sunday 9th [October]

Another pleasant morning. Last night I didn't feel well, this morning I feel better.

Monday 10th [October]

A bright warm morning. I have been quite busy to-day helping Libby cook, made some crackers and light bread.

Mr. Parker came from Fillmore to-day to go with us to California[,] brought a sack of nice cling Peaches, and some dried ones with him. We are preparing some for the remaining part of our trip.

Tuesday 11th [October]

A warm pleasant morning some cloudy like rain, but it rains so seldom here. I think it likely it will clear off without any, I wish it would rain enough to lay the dust.

Cleared off without any rain, a beautiful moonlight night.

Wednesday 12th [October]

Another pretty morning, been busy all day helping Libby.

It has been very warm all day. Now it is cool and pleasant, and a bright moonlight night.

Thursday 13th [October]

A cool pleasant morning. The Dr. and a number of others have gone to Fillmore this morning, will not return till tomorrow.

I feel truly thankful to my Heavenly Parent for all his tender mercies for my returning health. Oh may I ever praise his Adorable Name.

The Dr. & Mr. Parker Got back from Fillmore about 10 o'clock to-night.

Friday 14th [October]

A bright pleasant morning but rather cold. Was busy today making Crackers.

Saturday 15th [October]

About cool enough for a frost this morning.

I have been busy today helping Elizabeth, feel about tuckered out. Oh how I wish I felt well. But I feel thankful that I am as well as I am.

The 1864 Diary of Mrs. Sarah Jane Rousseau

Sunday 16th [October]

A cool clear morning.

I feel ashamed to acknowledge how unprofitable I have spent this Sabbath day. Have been busy all day cooking[,] helping Libby. I hope the time will soon come when I can spend the Sabbath in a more acceptable way.

Monday 17th [October]

This morning cold and frosty. A while after sun up it got warm and pleasant. I have been busy all day cooking and mending old clothes.

The Indian Chief Kanoss came early this morning and told us he heard the Indians above on Muddy Creek were very troublesome. A few weeks ago there were five of their number killed by the whites, and they are determined [on] having revenge. I am afraid we may have trouble with them when we get where we are [going].

Tuesday 18th [October]

A cold but pleasant morning.

Last night the Dr. Messrs. Earp, Curtis Hamilton met at Mr. Hatton's for the purpose of reorganizing our company for the remaining part of our journey from Petersburg (commonly called Corn Creek) to Southern California. Writing down certain regulations to be governed by. All that go in our train with us shall sign their names or go in some other way.

I have not felt well all day, notwithstanding I have been busy all day helping Libby, she has been washing up the dirty clothes as we intend starting on Thursday.

Wednesday 19th [October]

A cold frosty morning.

Some of the companies said there was an earthquake last night, they felt it, thought they heard the rumbling of a waggon. Was thought to be the shock of an Earth Quake. I didn't hear it or feel it.

Thursday 20th [October]

Quite cold and frosty this morning. Last night another shock of Earth Quake was felt.
This morning all confusion getting ready for another start. Got ready about 10 o'clock and bid farewell to Corn Creek. The appearance of the country now seems to have had considerable volcanic action by the quantity of rocks that have been thrown up. It has a strange appearance.

We traveled on and got to what is called Baker's Pass, 12 miles, to Dog Valley Kanyon where we camped, rather pretty place.

(Went 12 miles to-day.)

Friday 21st [October]

Started from camp quite early. It is a freezing cold morning.

Passed Dog Valley Kanyon, over a mountain. Got to Cove Creek about noon, took on water, crossed Pine Creek, ascended a high mountain called Pine Valley Mountain, made a dry camp on its summit. A very pretty place to camp[,] 16 miles. (18 miles.)

Saturday 22nd [October]

Another cold morning.

Started from camp about 7 o'clock. Descended through Wild Cat Cañon. Went over a mountain, a pretty bad one to get up, through Beaver Valley[,] quite a pretty Valley[.] Came to Beaver, the county seat of Beaver County, a distance of 18 miles.

Here we have camped for a short time, being obliged to have some tires made smaller, horse shoeing and milling done. Beaver is a small place, not pretty, most of the houses low Adobe buildings.

Made 13 miles to-day.

Sunday 23rd [October]

A cold cloudy morning[.] But it has cleared off and quite windy. I fear we will have some trouble with Mr. Earp, his refusing to take the Dr.'s box of books any farther than this place, says he can't[,] being so heavy loaded[.]

The arrangement was for him to take them through to California for him. It seems we can't place any dependence in what he says. We can't take them[,] being heavier loaded than any of them. I don't know how they will do yet, the Dr. says he will have to take it or give up the horses and oxen that belong to us.

Monday 24th [October]

A cold cloudy morning[.] Last night it commenced raining and continued to rain all night. It is very cold yet.

I suffered a good deal of pain in my back last night. I hope I'll feel better when it clears off warm and pleasant. I suppose we will be ready to start by to-morrow at noon. I am anxious to get into warmer climate.

I went over to-day to see Mrs. Hatten, Earp and Hamilton. While at Mrs. Hamilton's we had a hard hail storm. I was weather bound, had to stay there till after dinner. We were all pretty near frozen to death[.]

Towards night[,] it became much calmer and more pleasant.

Tuesday 25th [October]

This morning is very cold and unpleasant. It blowed hard a while before day, hailed and snowed.

It is still snowing and blowing pretty hard, but has the appearance of clearing. I have been obliged to stay in the carriage to keep as warm as possible. I suffer a great deal with pain in my back and hips. I think it likely the stormy weather makes me worse. I hope before many days we will be in a warmer climate[.] By tomorrow morning[,] I think we will be ready to proceed on our journey.

Wednesday 26th [October]

A very cold morning[,] the ground frozen, the sun is now making all things appear bright and pleasant. I think we will have a pleasant day[,] it is all calm and serene. We are now preparing for another start.

Left camp about 9 o'clock[,] passed through Beaver Cañon then went 3 miles from the summit and camped. Traveled 13 miles.

I suffered a great deal to-day with cold[.] The mountains, the high ones[,] are covered with snow which makes it pretty cold in the Vallies. (Made 13 miles.)

Thursday 27th [October]

Got up very early. I should think about 2 o'clock. Started from camp a little after sun up. A cold freezing morning. Heated some irons to keep my feet warm. Was comfortable all day.

Went 7 miles to Buck Horn Springs, from there 8 miles to Little Creek, 2 miles farther to Red Cr. Patagonia, not a very large place, has some larger buildings than in Beaver.

Came 17 miles to-day. (Mr. Curtis is quite sick with the fever, the Dr. is attending to him.)

Friday 28th [October]

Rather cloudy, snowed a little while, not as cold as yesterday. About ready to start from camp.

It has been growing colder all day. 4 miles came to Parawan. Had a view of Salt Lake West of Parawan, 6 miles to Summit Creek, six miles to Johnson's Fort, rather a nice camping place[.] We intend staying till morning.

Traveled 16 miles to-day. (Parawan is quite a pretty place. Much larger buildings than we have seen in general in the small towns.)

Saturday 29th [October]

A very cold morning, last night was extremely cold. I went to see Mrs. Curtis[,] appeared some better, the sun is shining bright at this time which makes it much more pleasant. Nearly ready to start from camp[.]

Left camp about 8 o'clock, traveled 6 miles to Cedar City, passed by 2 miles and camped. We had not been here more than 2 hours when a heavy wind arose, about blew our tent down, then it commenced snowing[.] We all suffered with the cold. Could hardly finish getting our dinner ready, but it got ready before a great while, after a fashion.

There appears to be a storm coming now. The clouds almost cover the Mountains at this time.

It looks desolate and dreary, most of the mountains are covered with snow. The Dr. has gone to buy some grain for the horses to take them through to California.

Came 8 miles to-day. (Cedar City. We are now 100 miles from Corn Cr. Sent a letter to Mary Ann 31st of October.)

Sunday 30th [October]

Last night about midnight blow a hard wind and snowed all night.

This morning still snowing and pretty cold. It looks very dreary and desolate, did not leave camp on account of bad weather. I suppose we will leave in the morning if the weather is favorable.

Monday 31st [October]

A cold morning and snowing hard. It commenced in the night to snow and blow, and kept on till about three this afternoon, when the sun gave a gleam of light through the clouds. It gladdens our hearts considerable. It still has the appearance of clearing off.

The horses, poor things, suffer with the cold. I feel sorry to see them. I hope it will clear so we can leave camp in the morning.

Tuesday 1st [November]

Last night cleared off[,] very cold. This morning freezing cold. Think we better travel to-day and get to where it's warmer as soon as we can.

Left camp pretty late this morning. Went 16 miles to-day.

Wednesday 2nd [November]

A cold morning but not as cold as yesterday. Left camp about sun up, went to Pinto Creek, watered our horses then went on to Pinto[,] a distance of 10 miles and camped.

10 miles to-day.

This is a rather small town and pretty. Appears to be a new place[,] most of the building low Adobes, some few log houses.

The 1864 Diary of Mrs. Sarah Jane Rousseau

Thursday 3rd [November]

Quite cool this morning, intend laying over to-day.

Libby washed some to-day. After sun up it turned warm and pleasant.

Friday 4th [November]

This morning bright and clear. Some warmer than it has been, making preparations to leave camp.

Started rather late[,] after nine o'clock. Went from Pinto to Mountain Meadows where we camped. There we saw a monument erected to the memory of the dead. It made me awful sick at heart to look at it and think of the suffering of the poor emigrants which was cruelly massacred at this place, Mountain Meadows.

This train of emigrants, a mixed one, some from Michigan, some from Indiana, some from other states. They arrived here in September '57 where they were murdered in cold blood by the Mormons. There was is a monument raised to their memory once before, but the Mormons tore it down.

This spring[,] some time in May, some soldiers came through from California, and erected this Monument and dared any of the Mormons to touch it. There was 150 cruelly butchered men, women and children, only 6 small children too young to tell the tale were suffered to live. They are at Salt Lake City.

I cannot for a moment suppose that such barbarism will be buried in Oblivion. "Oh, it cannot be." It will be brought to light and the aggressors punished.

We have passed the Rim of the Basin and are now on the Waters of the Colorado where we will soon be in warmer climate. All through here is broken and mountainous. Made 12 miles.

Saturday 5th [November]

Quite a cool morning. Commenced guarding last night. We are now in a part of the country where we may have to contend with the Indians. There will be danger of them for a hundred miles. I hope we'll get safe through.

Left camp[,] went two miles to Cane Springs, where we watered the horses and eat a luncheon. Then started over a rough, rocky, mountainous road to Santa Clara Creek, where we watered our horses again and filled our kegs with water, as there is none to get for some distance[.]

Went on about mile and half and then camped. A real nice place, plenty of wood. There was quite a difference in the atmosphere after we got there, it was warm and pleasant. Made 10 miles to-day.

Sunday 6th [November]

A pleasant morning[,] much warmer than it has been for some time.

Started from camp a while after sun up, traveled over very rough roads. We are in Diamond Valley where we have stopped to water the horses at Diamond Valley Springs. The Dr. and Mr. Parker have gone to the top of the mountain close by to look at a Volcano. I looked up while writing this and saw them both at the top.

There has been great Volcanic action of the Earth all along where we are traveling. It appears if all Nature had been disturbed and moved. The immense quantity of melted rock[,] as it appears to me[,] that have been thrown up, rocks of great magnitude that have been moved from their resting place[,] that we can behold and acknowledge the wonderful works of an Almighty God.

When the horses got back[,] we started on. We are in a part of the country the Mormons call Dixie. And a more rough, rugged, rough, mountainous country cannot be found. We passed by some Volcanic Mountains, the effects of which we saw for miles. The Lava that has been thrown out looks like cinders. The mountains some of them have a grand appearance, some a red color, while others have a white appearance. Some of them[,] I think must be four hundred feet high.

This Cañon is called Diamond. At the mouth[,] it takes us into Santa Clara Valley which we traveled through & down a pretty dangerous hill to Santa Clara Creek where we camped pretty close to a Ranch called Hamblin's Ranch where we got good feed and shelter for our horses.

There came a number of Piute Indians. They are a tribe that is very fond of horse flesh to eat, and great hands to steal anything they can lay their hands on. We have come to-day 20 miles.

Monday 7th [November]

Started from camp late this morning. It is a cold windy time. The Dr. had to prescribe and deal out medicine for a little child that belonged to a Mormon Bishop. About breakfast time[,] a number of Indians came to the camp and we gave them their breakfast.

When we started[,] four of them started with us[,] three of them on foot and one [on] horseback. They are miserable looking creatures, some of them almost destitute of clothing. I believe it is their intention to go to the Muddy with us. As for me[,] I would rather have their doom than their company. I am afraid of them.

We have crossed the Clara fifteen times this morning, a real disagreeable time. Made 5 miles.

Tuesday 8th [November]

A cold blustery morning, the wind blew hard all night.

Started from camp rather late with an escort of from 10 to 15 Piute Indians. Last night[,] two of them stayed with us as prisoners. Our guide Mr. Hatten said it would not do to let them leave camp after dark, as they might get some other indians, come back and do us some mischief.

We started from camp with five[,] which increased to fifteen of them. We crossed the Santa Clara this morning 16 times and after going 12 miles at Camp Springs, having filled our kegs [at] the last crossing place. The Indian Chief told the guide we must all give them something for traveling through their country, to renumerate them for the using [of] wood, water & grass. We all gave them some flour.

We intend to let them have the care of our horses to-night, they are going to take the cattle as well. The Chief with four others we keep as prisoners till morning when they bring back the stock. Then they will be free.

The 1864 Diary of Mrs. Sarah Jane Rousseau

(Made 12 miles to-day. We are in the Arizona territory.)

Wednesday 9th [November]

A pretty morning. Started from camp about sun up.

The Indians brought the stock safe back, left camp with our escort, traveled over some rough road till noon.
This afternoon[,] the road much better, passed over the summit between the Clara and the Virgin, went 5 miles in the cañon and camped. Some grass for the stock but no water.

Came 13 miles to-day.

Thursday 10th [November]

A cool but pleasant morning. Last night[,] the Indians were prisoners again. They let the stock go on the mountains to feed. We fed five among us, all are willing to do so but Mr. Earp. He swears and cuts up about it, although he derives the same benefit as the rest of us. I fear he may cause us some trouble when we get to the Muddy.

We went over some rough roads this morning and stopped to noon in the cañon as some of the cattle gave out.

Started on again[.] The roads were a good deal better this afternoon. Traveled on until we came to Beaver Creek, where the stock drank bountifully of the crystal stream, haven't had but little water to quench their thirst since we left the Clara. We filled the kegs there and had to water them out of them.

Saw some curious looking trees. One of the Indians said the name of them was Chaurarran. They are a curious looking tree[.] The leaves has the appearance of Porcupine Quills.

Before we got down to the creek[,] we felt a great difference in the atmosphere[.] Much warmer and more pleasant. When we got to the Creek, the trees looked like early Autumn, quite reviving to one[']s feelings after suffering with the cold so much.

About 2 hours before we got there[,] an old indian died[.] When we arrived they were burning him up. That is the way they put their dead out of sight. They dig a hole about a foot deep in their Wicky up, put the body in, and burn all up together. It is indeed a heathenish way to get the dead out of their sight.

We have rather a pretty camping place, plenty of wood, water and grass. The Indians have the care of our stock at night, which we pay them for. They have proven faithful as yet[,] taking them where there is good grass.

(Made 18 miles to-day. We are in New Mexico.)

Friday 11th [November]

A calm beautiful morning[.] Intend laying over to-day. Our guide Mr. Hatten had a bad chill in the night, he was real sick this morning. The

Dr. gave him some medicine. I hope he will be able to go in the morning.

The women have all been busy washing & baking to-day. Making ready for another start.

Saturday 12th [November]

Another pretty morning, warm and pleasant[.] Have to lay over on account of our guide not feeling able to travel.

Did some more washing to-day, washing and baking and various other things. It is a very warm day.

Sunday 13th [November]

A pleasant warm morning[,] some cooler than yesterday. Mr. Hatten is a good deal better[.]

We are now preparing for another start. The Indians have been faithful with the stock. They are all here this morning. Started from Beaver Creek at sun up, had to go up a deep sandy hill, had to double teams, and then it was so hard to get up. Went on to the Virgin River, and crossed 18 times, the road is very rough.

It is a wild looking country, seemingly nothing but a sandy desert, high Beaver looking mountains on both sides. The poor horses almost gave out going over such bad roads.

Got to a camping place about three this afternoon. All the Indians left us but one. We told them if they went on they would have to find their own provisions, we had given them all we could.

Came 18 miles.

Monday 14th [November]

A pleasant morning[,] making ready to leave camp.

Started late[.] Some of the stock was missing. After so long a time[,] went on, traveled over some rough roads. Crossed the Virgin 9 times. Camped about sun down.

Our company got separated[.] Some of them chose to stay on a swampy piece of ground. We preferred crossing the river and camp on dry sand. Mr. Hamilton, Jesse Curtis and Tom Hays & ourselves camped on dry sand.

Came 15 miles.

Tuesday 15th [November]

This morning quite cool.

Some of the company didn't appear to like our crossing the river to another camping place. We think Mr. Earp was the cause of our guide camping in such a sickly place. He seems as if he was to make hard feelings among us. This morning[,] they passed by and left us. But we soon caught up with them.

We had to cross the Virgin five or six times. When the guide crossed and got fast in a Quick Sand[,] had to have help to get out. One of the oxen got down in a quick sand and like[ly] to have got drowned[.]

Going back after the waggon they left behind[,] when within 4 miles where we camped on the hill ahead of there[,] there was ten Indians with their guns[,] bows & arrows watching us. The Indian that came with us from Beaver named Frank[,] went up the hill to them. After ascending the hill[,] all the coloured tribe followed us to the camping grounds.

The Chief is [a] quite good looking Indian, his name Tooso. Could speak English pretty well. Our guide made arrangements with him to have some of his Indians to herd the stock and we could pay him. The Indians old and young that stayed at the camp numbered 14. Through Mr. Hatten's influence with them[,] we have got along pretty well, he passed us all off as Mormons.

The growth of Timber along the Virgin is mostly Willow, some Cottonwood & a pretty looking bush called Muskete, some Sage & grease wood, the appearance of the Bush at this time is like early fall.

We crossed the river to-day 11 times. (Made 15 miles to-day.)

Wednesday 16th [November]

This morning cool & cloudy.

The 1864 Diary of Mrs. Sarah Jane Rousseau

Last night it clouded up, blowed hard, and rained most of the night. This morning it hailed, is still cloudy but not falling weather.

Left camp about 8 o'clock, looked out of the carriage just now and saw some of the mountains covered with snow.

Got to our last crossing place on the Virgin, rather dangerous on account of quick sands. The guide has crossed, I don't know how the rest of us will get along, some have to double teams.

All have got across safe. We have crossed three times this morning, and are now ready to ascend Virgin hill. It looks to be an awful one to get up, some say it is six miles long.

We are now on the top of the hill or rather Mountain & I will acknowledge I never saw such a one, let alone ascend it. When we were below the worst part of it, I looked up and thought it was an utter impossibility for any animal to get up. Toward the top[,] there was a perpendicular rock some six feet to get up, beside some others not so bad. We all double teams but Mr. Earp's family waggon. He started up that awful mountain with our mare & Mr. Hamilton's horses, but the poor things couldn't make it. Mr. Hamilton started a pair of mules after them to help them along, they got up safe. It appears to me he didn't care if he killed our horses or not. If he had[,] he wouldn't [have] attempted to go up with only two.

All the Indians have traveled with us to-day[.]

It is very cold and has the appearance of snow. We are not farther enough South to escape winter weather. We must be four hundred feet above the Virgin. It looks very dreary. Nothing but mountains to be seen, and the growth [of] Wild Sage on the mountains where we have camped[.] That [is] we all have to gather to cook supper with. I suppose we will camp here as some of the stock have given out. It has taken us since 2 o'clock till nine at night to get all the waggons up.

Our poor horses have gone down the hill three times since bring our heavy waggon to help bringing those others up. It has been a dreadful time for them. It took 8 horses to get the large waggon up.

Made 10 miles.

Thursday 17th [November]

A very cold morning and the wind blowing hard. It was a cold windy night[.]

Left camp a little after sun up, and went on about five miles & camped[.] Still blowing hard & cold. The stock seem to be all worn out. We intend staying here till morning.

Made 5 miles to-day.

Friday 18th [November]

This morning very cold. Last night blowed a fair gale[.]

Left camp about 8 o'clock, went on to the Muddy about 10 miles, met some 30 to 40 Indians[,] large & small, watered our horses & ate a luncheon, went two miles farther and camped. The Indians all followed us. We all gave them something to eat & they herded the stock.

Saturday 19th [November]

Another cold morning, got a thick coat of ice out of the bucket. Yesterday in the middle of the day it was very warm[,] turned cold at night. We think of starting this morning on the big desert, about 58 miles through[.] We have to travel night & day till we are across, being nothing for the stock to eat or drink on the way. I dread it very much on account of the poor worn out stock.

The 1864 Diary of Mrs. Sarah Jane Rousseau

We are all busy cooking for the trip. We'll have to carry as much water as we can for the horses, and ourselves to make a little coffee. If we can make it across the desert[,] I think we'll be safe.

The water in the muddy is quite warm and has a Milky appearance, but when in a bucket it's clear. The growth on the river is Willow and Muskete[,] rather pretty stream.

Left camp half past two[.] The Indians stayed back[,] all but four[,] they follow on. Went up the cañon a gradual ascent till we got on the desert.

After sun down[,] stopped a while and fed the horses. Some of Mr. Curtis['] oxen gave out entirely.

It was our time to be [the] foot of the train today, Mr. Curtis next, their team stopped so often that the foremost waggon got a mile ahead of us & our horses being stopped so oft[,] it was an injury to them and we went on by them.

A young man traveling with Mr. Curtis went by on Horseback and stopped the train. By the time we got up with them[,] they had made several large fires. It was very cold. We were all pretty near frozen.

We waited till they all came up, rested the teams & went on till day break, stopped again and made fires.

Sunday 20th [November]

Concluded to have breakfast and feed the horses grain, still very cold. Here we are this sabbath morning on the desert, it has the right name. It is indeed a dreary looking wilderness.

At 9 o'clock[,] stopped again to feed & water the horses out of our kegs. Mr. Parker has been to the mountains making discoveries[.] Just returned[,] brought a pretty little bird back[,] perfectly preserved, it looks as if it was alive. I think it a Wren.

He brought some specimens of this production of the Earth. We suppose it to be Sulphate of lime. It is a pretty specimen and transparent.

The 1864 Diary of Mrs. Sarah Jane Rousseau

Now tis very warm. We are ready to start again, traveled until five in the afternoon, when we stopped to make some coffee and rest the horses, then went on till daybreak, when our horses in the carriage gave out entirely. Then the train passed by and left me and the children alone on the dessert, our big waggon had gone on.

I suppose we were alone an hour and half when Mr. Parker came on horseback to help us. The Dr. was sick and couldn't come. He hitched the horse he brought with one of ours and we rolled on, got to Las Vegas about 8 o'clock. Got our breakfast[.]

About 10 o'clock[,] four new teams came in. Had just crossed the desert. They left this afternoon. Mr. Hamilton's family went on with them. Mr. Parker went.

(58 miles across the desert.)

Monday 21st [November]

The Dr. very sick to-day. I feel pretty low spirited. Quite cold this morning, we think of remaining here for a few days to recruit our horses. The poor things are about worn out.

Las Vegas is a barren desolate looking place. I saw one farm house and field fenced. A place walled up for a Fort. There are plenty of Indians here.

I think Dr. some better this afternoon[.] Traveled 58 miles since Saturday two o'clock.

Tuesday 22nd [November]

A pleasant morning. Some warmer than it has been. Busy to-day helping cook while Libby is [doing the] washing.

The Dr. very sick all night, not any better this morning, cramps considerably, has been taking medicine. I hope he'll get better soon.

About night Dr. the felt better, got up and eat some.

Wednesday 23rd [November]

A cool cloudy morning. The Dr. rested pretty well last night, feels better this morning. Think will start from Camp after dinner. Intend going six miles.

Disappointed again, can't leave this afternoon on account of Mr. Curtis's mare getting mired.

I feel tolerable low spirited. The Dr. sick and we are pretty near out of all kinds of provisions, our means nearly exhausted. In a strange country almost out of money & but few friends.

Oh how dreary and desolate things appear to me. I must not, I dare not allow myself to think of our situation. Myself[,] almost helpless. But still I feel thankful that I am so much better than I was when I left home. I was then entirely helpless. Now[,] I can walk some & help a little about the work. Still I don't regret leaving home when I think of my restoration the health.

It has been a trying trip for all, and health ought to be prized above all things. If I regain my health, I shall always remember our journey with a thankful heart and give praise to our Heavenly Father for his tender mercies and continual watchfulness over us.

Thursday 24th [November]

This morning Mr. Earp had another rippet with Warren fighting with Jimmy Hatten and then he commenced about all the children. Used very profane language & swore if the children's parents did not whip or correct their children, he would whip every last one of them. He still shows us more and more every day what kind of a man he is.

Friday 25th [November]

Another clear pleasant morning, but cool.

Making ready to leave camp, have plenty of indians around all the time. I am tired out seeing them.

Mr. Earp has just given up our box of books, says he can't take them any farther. So we'll leave them at this place to be taken by some freighters [at] the first opportunity.

Charlie Capley has left Mr. Earp and [is] going the remaining part of the way with us.

Mr. Curtis's mare so used up he can't take her on, he sold her for fifteen dollars.

Started[,] went 4 miles & camped. Plenty of grass, sage wood & water, heard the frogs croaking all night. It made me think of spring.

To-day was warm and pleasant, evening and morning are cool, after sun up it is generally warmer, some times too warm. The Dr. feels some better to-night.

Saturday 26th [November]

Cool and rather cloudy morning.
Left camp a little after sun up, traveled all day over very rough roads & up hill all the way, got to Cottonwood spring where we camped, a tolerable good camping place. Before we got there[,] one of the mares gave out[,] Fan, had to put another on.

It was pleasant and warm all day. At night it blew very hard. I was afraid the carriage would blow over, it did go down hill a piece. The Dr. got up to fix it when he discovered Mr. Curtis's tent in flames, just in time to save him from being burnt up. He and a young man[4] were sound asleep in the tent. The Dr. went and pulled one of them by the leg, thought it was one of the children which soon awoke them. They got up in a hurry[,] that's certain. Their bed badly burned and an old quilt. The guard[,] instead of putting the fire out[,] was so windy[,] was making one.

Made 20 miles to-day.

---

[4] Previously identified as Mack.

Sunday 27th [November]

A warm but cloudy [morning.] The wind abated some.

Started from camp rather late, went on 6 miles to William's Ranch where we camped at the mouth of the cañon. Soon after we got there it began to blow and commenced to rain. I think I never saw such a bothersome night in my life. It blew a fair hurricane without any interruption.

We all suffered very much with the cold and pretty near drowned, lying soaking wet all night. It leaked through the roof of the carriage, a thing it had never done before.

Monday 28th [November]

At last the wished for morning came, the wind had abated. By sun up it cleared up considerably[.]

Left camp about ten o'clock, traveled on through the mountain roads. At last the two grey mares in the carriage gave out, couldn't go any farther. By this time the train had gone a good way. Our big waggon was along with them.

At last[,] Mack missed us[.] Came to see what [was] the matter. He had to get the teams in our big waggon and came after us.

At last we reached Mountain Springs where we camped. Made 12 miles to-day.

Tuesday 29th [November]

This morning very cold, the ground froze.

Left camp at 9 o'clock. Traveled on to Stump Springs over a rough, rugged looking country, a perfect desert, the weather still cold but not cold enough to freeze.

The roads were very good to-day, we got along very well. Traveled 18 miles to-day.

Wednesday 30th [November]

Another cold morning. Had to let Tom Hays have the carriage to take through to San Bernardino, California for us, our horses too much tuckered out to go in it. We left it at Stump Springs.

I have to go in the big waggon. It is harder for me, but if we only get through safe I shall feel glad. My health is much improved.

Traveled over some bad roads to-day[,] up hill most of the way, had to fill our kegs with water[.]

Traveled about 15 miles and made a dry camp, better camping place than last night. The horses got along better than I thought they would. The poor children have to walk most of the time. Made 15 miles.

Thursday 1st [December]

A bright sun shiny morning & quite cool. Making for another start.

Left camp about 8 o'clock[.] Went over some rough roads[,] rocky roads & over a high mountain, almost as bad as the Virgin. Went on a few miles farther to Resting Springs where we have camped, plenty of good grass and water but a scarcity of wood.

Here[,] we met with our Indian friends. I had hopes we had seen the last of them.

We will stay a day or two here[,] making preparation to cross the desert, making and baking bread. That's about all we will have to do. Our provisions all about used up except a little rice & sugar which I intend cooking.

It has been a hard day for me[,] the roads so rough, my feet pain me considerable. Made 18 miles.

The 1864 Diary of Mrs. Sarah Jane Rousseau

Friday 2nd [December]

A pleasant morning.

In looking around me while riding I see nothing but mountains & broken country. Oh how dreary and desolate. If we cross the desert in safety, we shall then reach civilization.

Last night I heard the frog[s] croaking. This is Elizabeth's birthday, 15 years old. Spent it at Resting Springs, I believe California.

Saturday 3rd [December]

A pleasant morning, rather cool, intend leaving camp after breakfast.

The 1864 Diary of Mrs. Sarah Jane Rousseau

Started about 8 o'clock, had to leave our company back on account of Mrs. Curtis sick and couldn't travel. We[,] in a case of necessity[,] was obliged to go. We were out of feed for our horses and our family.

[**Editorial note**: Several words appear to have been erased from this section. The editor has used conjecture to fill in the blanks. These are marked with underlining.]

> The Dr. asked if others would share from their feed to carry them through, *a request that* no one couldn't do. I am surprised as we have been through so much for them to refuse us now. Their actions speak louder than the agreement we had all made.

The 1864 Diary of Mrs. Sarah Jane Rousseau

<u>We have tried everything to make the work light for our poor horses.</u> The Dr. tried the test of Mr. Earp at Stump Springs by asking if he couldn't take our empty waggon along [with] loose horses, and he thought it would be easier on the horses than the boys racing through all creation.

Our leaving them this morning was a case of necessity or starve ourselves and the horses. We are now at the last Watering Place till we cross the desert, having to fill all our kegs here. It is a spring on the Armagosa River. Started on and went over some very bad Rocks[,] Sand & Hills. Language is almost inadequate to describe the utter desolation & barrenness of this great wilderness.

The 1864 Diary of Mrs. Sarah Jane Rousseau

We went on until within 2 ½ miles of Salt Springs, when our poor jaded horses stopped, couldn't go any farther. Oh how I pitied them. We took them out and made a dry camp. Made 20 miles today.

Sunday 4th [December]

A pretty morning but rather cool.

Geared up and started, the horses couldn't pull the waggon through the sand. We unloaded some and I got out, took one more out and put another in her place. I got on the one they took out and rode to the camping place.

Here is a dilapidated looking place, 4 houses besides a quartz mill. Has been destroyed[,] it is said[,] by the Indians. There must have been some thousands expended to fix for getting gold. We are informed there was three men left here to take care of the property, when some Indians came and killed them about 8 weeks ago. The destruction of things seems a pity[:] stones, buckets, iron & all that is needed for such a Mill.

I suppose in the morning we will start on the desert. Came 2 ½ miles.

Monday 5th [December]

A very pleasant morning[.] Preparing for leaving camp to try our luck on crossing the desert. I suppose we will be ready by sun up.

Started from camp at 7 o'clock with our three span of poor horses, traveled on till noon, stopped to rest, feed & water the horses. Got along better than I expected so far. Eat our dinner[,] some bread & a little meat, the last meat we have.

Went until sun down[,] gave the horses a little feed and rested them two hours.

Started on again intending to travel on till the moon went down, but the horses gave out entirely. We had to take them out & camp. The horse we call Charlie[,] when he was taken out of the waggon[,] staggered and would have fallen had not a young man that was with us[5] taken hold of him and steadied him.

When we stopped[,] it was about ten o'clock. Made about 23 miles.

---
[5] Charle Capley (see November 25).

Tuesday 6th [December]

Got up ¼ past four [in the morning]. It Is a very pleasant morning. Intend as soon as breakfast is over to make another effort to go through. We could only put in four horses this morning[,] the other three can't work. We gave the poor things their last feed of barley.

Oh how my heart aches to see them, they look like skeletons & so pitiful[,] begging something to eat. They try to eat the dry brush or any thing they can get hold of. We went about three miles when they stopped, couldn't travel any farther.

My poor little children have walked most of the way. And now how desolate we feel. We had to let the poor little boys go with Mack & the horses to Bitter Springs where there may be some grass that may save the poor things from starving to death.

What bitter tears I have shed to think of our condition. Here in the wild desert with a small quantity of flour, enough with care to last a few days. While Charlie Capley & Richard Curtis have gone on foot traveling night & day till they reach Mojave River, get a team if they can, and some provisions to help us through. While writing this there is a small gleam of hope in our hearts. The Dr. discovered a train at a distance coming. Oh how I hope there may be help for us in this[,] our time of need. If Mr. Cutis had only let us have had one bushel of barley[,] we might have got through safe. Our horses are perfectly healthy but about starving to death.

The train came[.] It was our train. He saw I.C. Curtis and told him our condition and told him he would like to have him take Libby and myself if he could. Mr. C. made answer and said he couldn't take us, they were so heavy loaded & were out of provisions & their teams pretty much tuckered out.

At last they got here and although they know I could hardly walk on smooth ground and this is very rocky, yet none of the women came near me to ask how I got along, but past by as if I had done something amiss. Mrs. C. was hauled along in our carriage, the one I.C. Curtis refused.

Well they stopped a rod or two above us and eat their suppers. I suppose they got to thinking all things over and got ashamed. Curtis and Earp came to us. Curtis made a proposition that he would try and take Libby and I and partake of their fare, but he was very much crowded and was afraid his teams would give out. I thanked him kindly for his offer & concluded to stay with my husband.

Mr. Earp made a similar offer. I answered him about the same as I did Mr. Curtis, saying I would be obliged to ride all the way & that would be additional weight for their teams and we had sent on to the Mojave to get teams to take us through, thanked him for the offer he made but I would rather stay here a few days till they came after us. So they went on a few miles intending to camp in the cañon.

(Mrs. Curtis had a fine daughter while at Resting Springs, her and the babe are doing well.)

Wednesday 7th [December]

A beautiful morning. Warm and pleasant. The Butterflies and flies are bussing around. All nature is bright around us, but I feel gloomy and desolate.

My dear little boys away from us, our poor horses[,] we don't know whether they would be able to go where they could get something to eat, or have to starve to death in this wild desert but I try to keep up my spirits as well as I can under such circumstances.

The Dr. feels so bad[.] I don't want to make him feel any worse than he does by my taking on. I will put my trust in the Lord. I think all things will work together for our good if we will only have faith. It is four years ago to-day since I bid father Rousseau farewell, on my returning home to Iowa from the southern part of Ky. It was just such a pleasant day as this, quite warm.

Thursday 8th [December]

A beautiful warm morning[.] See or hear nothing but a Raven that has sit close by us. No appearance of any train yet.

Last night nothing came to disturb our slumbers.

Friday 9th [December]

A very pleasant morning.

We had gone to bed last night and was aroused from our sleep by hearing the tramp of horses feet coming this way. The Dr. jumped up in a hurry to listen and soon discovered two men & two span of horses coming toward the waggon & found out sure enough it was Charlie Capley & another gentleman by the name of Lindsay had come after us & glad we were to see them.

They brought some flour, beans & molasses which were very acceptable. Libby and I jumped up and cooked them some supper as soon as possible. They told us they saw Mack & the boys. They were getting along very well, they had five horses along, the other three they couldn't get along. They brought horse feed along with them, left them some bread & barley for the horses they had along.

They stopped at Bitter Springs & saw the horses Charlie & Flit, but Fan they did not see. They gave them a good feed and started. When they got within eight miles of where we camped[,] they saw poor Fan dead on the desert[,] starve to death. If we had only have had a little feed[,] we could have saved our horses.

(Made 35 miles to-day. Mr. Lindsey said the reason they hurried [was] the gentleman at the Ranch said there was danger from Indians making an attack, if they should find out we were there alone.)

The 1864 Diary of Mrs. Sarah Jane Rousseau

*Saturday 10th [December][6]

Got up ¼ past four. A very pleasant morning. Got ready by sun up & started from camp[.]

Passed by poor Fan. She was pretty much eat up with the wolves. Went on to Bitter Springs, where we saw poor Flit down & couldn't get up. The Dr. tried to raise her, but she fell down on her mouth. She tried to raise again[,] but fell on her side, she fairly tore ground and tried to bite it. The Dr. then took his revolver and shot her to put an end to her misery.

---

[6] Previously published versions of the diary list this as another entry for July 9. This error, perpetuated with continuously wrong dating moving forward, provides an inaccurate date of arrival of the Rousseau family's in San Bernardino, California. Corrective dates are marked with an asterisk.

Oh how bad I felt for the poor things[,] to think what a hard summer they had & then to starve to death. We did not know that Charlie would meet the same fate. He looked awful bad[.] We fed him and stayed about three hours to cook our own dinner & cook bread enough to take us across the desert, then got ready & went on[,] resting a good many times.

The roads were dreadful bad, a great deal of heavy sand[.] One hill we had to go up was twenty miles & sand all the way, very hard on the poneys. The men walked all the way.

We still traveled on till three in the morning, then camped tired enough. Met the old gentleman that keeps the ranch about 30 miles from Bitter Springs with some more grain for the horses & a mule if we should need it to put it in with the ponies. One of the ponies appeared more tired than the rest and they put the mule in for a while. Made 25 miles to-day.

*Sunday 11th [December]

Got up about sun up[,] rather cool. Started from camp about ½ past 7. The roads bad but better than yesterday[,] being down hill most of the way.
After a tedious travel[,] arrived at Mojave River at 3 P.M. The train having just got in the night before. They all came to see us and appeared glad we had got through.

*Monday 12th [December]

A pretty warm morning.

Mr. Lindsey and his company left this morning for San Bernardino. Earps think of leaving in the morning. I hope we can leave in a day or so.

*Tuesday 13th [December]

A warm but cloudy morning. The train left this morning for San Bernardino[,] leaving us here. We leave in the morning.
We had to hire [a] team to take us through, leave our horses here till we send our waggon back with a load for the gentleman that keeps the Ranch.

The Dr. is attending to a young man about to die, a son of Mr. Allcorn. He appears some better than he was. They seem real clever people, the old gentleman is from Kentucky, his wife from North Carolina. They are Seceshionist.

It is now a sun shiny day[,] quite warm. Libby is washing. I have been trying to cook a little.

*Wednesday 14th [December]

A cool cloudy morning, raining some, has the appearance of raining considerably. We have to lay over another day for a span of mules to come in from San Bernardino to put in with the ponies. We expect they will be here some time to-day.

We have been treated very kindly since we came here.

It is now raining fast. There has been a good deal of rain lately in the settlement. The people seem to rejoice a good deal about it. It has been so dry for a year or two, some of the inhabitants have lost 10 or 20 thousand head of stock from starvation.

*Thursday 15th [December]

Started from camp[,] the Mojave[,] by sun up. Cool and cloudy. It rained about all day yesterday. We got some freighters to let us have enough team to take us through to San Bernardino. I hope we will be there in a day or two.

The roads were some better than they have been sometimes, although quite sandy, the rain did a great deal of good.

The 1864 Diary of Mrs. Sarah Jane Rousseau

(Made 18 miles to-day. To Grape Vine.)

*Friday 16th [December]

A clear frosty morning. Got up between 3 & 4[,] want to start from camp early. There is a Prussian [who] keeps the Ranch, his name Jacob. He lives most of the time alone. It is a lonesome looking place. I suppose we will get up with our train to-night, heard the Wolves last night.

Got up with our train. Em and Eliza came over to see Libby[,] they had some singing. There is a very cold wind blowing. This is Nicholson's Ranch, the old woman got drunk on whiskey. It is called Point of Rocks, a desolate looking place. Made 22 miles to-day.

The 1864 Diary of Mrs. Sarah Jane Rousseau

*Saturday 17th [December]

A cold cloudy morning. Started from camp before daylight. The roads rough & hilly. Went on to a ranch 14 miles from where we started in the morning, eat our lunch and fed the horses.

Started on to the Cedars where we camped. It was in the night when we got there, very cold & cloudy. Very soon it commenced raining and turned into snowing. The wind blew very hard[,] it is a real stormy night. Made 24 miles.

*Saturday 18th [December]

A very cold freezing morning, the ground covered with snow.

The 1864 Diary of Mrs. Sarah Jane Rousseau

Started from camp about an hour before day, got to the top of the Sierra Nevada Mountains by daylight. From the foot of the mountains to the top is 22 miles. Then we went down a very steep hill. It is down hill all the way to San Bernardino.

We are a way above the clouds this morning. It looks quite singular. We are now at Martin's Ranch. The appearance of the country is quite different from what it has been for some time back, every thing has a green lively look. The grass [is] growing nicely. It looks like spring instead of the middle of winter.

Got into San Bernardino about sun down. We heard Mr. Hamilton is 12 miles in the country on a farm. I don't know yet whether we will remain here or not. I haven't seen the town yet[,] don't know how it looks. I wish to get settled down.

Dr. James A. Rousseau's portrait, circa 1869 (Molony Family Collection) and Advertisement in *The Guardian*, January 11, 1868 (page 3).

The 1864 Diary of Mrs. Sarah Jane Rousseau

Mrs. Sarah J. Rousseau's portrait, circa 1869 (Molony Family Collection) and Advertisement in *The Guardian*, July 11, 1868 (page 3).

The 1864 Diary of Mrs. Sarah Jane Rousseau

For Further Reading

Anderson, Evalyn. "Anderson History." Essay, Grinnell: Marion-Linn D.A.R. Chapter of Iowa, 1934.

Campbell, J. L. *Idaho. Six Months in the New Gold Diggings: The Emigrant's Guide Overland.* Chicago: Campbell, 1864.

Cataldo, Nicholas R. "Curtis Family Legacy Began on a Wagon Train." *Pioneer Tales,* vol. 4, no. 3, 2020.

Cataldo, Nicholas R. "Diary of the Earp Wagon Train." *The Tombstone Epitaph*, November 27, 2019: 7.

Cataldo, Nicholas R. *Pioneers of San Bernardino 1851-1857.* San Bernardino: San Bernardino County Museum Association, 2001.

Cataldo, Nicholas R. "Sarah Jane Rousseau: Diary of the Earp Wagon Train to San Bernardino." *San Bernardino Sun,* 1999.

Cataldo, Nicholas R. *The Earp Clan: The Southern California Years*. San Bernardino: Backroads Press, 2006.

Cataldo, Nicholas R. "The Rousseau Diary and the Earp Wagon Train to San Bernardino, 1864." *Overland Journal* 33, no. 3 (2015): 115-129.

Cataldo, Nicholas R. "This pioneer's diary details cross-country trip to San Bernardino." *San Bernardino Sun*. March 21, 2022.

Daglish, Steven. "Sarah Jane Daglish - Trip Across The Plains." The Daglish Family (Blog), June 9, 2007. http://daglishfamily.blogspot.com/2007/06/sarah-jane-daglish-trip-across-plains.html

"Diary Tells of 1864 Trek by Covered Wagons." *San Bernardino Sun-Telegram*, November 21, 1954, 26.

Earp, Nicholas J. "Copy of a Handwritten Letter From Nicholas Earp to James Coplea," Pella Community Memory Database, Pella Public Library [Identifier: 2019.1.62.11], April 2, 1864.

Greenwood, Pamela. "Some Thoughts on the Pella Expedition." Genealogical Essay, December, 2006.

Molony, Janelle. "1864: More than Massacres." *Annals of Wyoming* (Autumn 2021): 30-47.

Molony, Janelle. "A Day in the Life with Sarah Rousseau." Janelle Molony Official Author Page. Last modified, March 31, 2020. http://janellemolony.com/category/rousseau-project/a-day-in-the-life-with-sarah-rousseau

Molony, Janelle, *Emigrant Tales of the Platte River Raids.* (Phoenix: M Press Publishing, 2023).

Molony, Janelle. "How a Victorian Immigrant Almost Became the First Lady." *The Michigan Historical Review* 48, no.1 (2022): 131-139.

Molony, Janelle. "Sarah Jane Daglish: A Case of Mistaken Identity." *The Stars In Your Family* (Burbank: Southern California Genealogical Society, 2021).

Molony, Janelle. "Victorian Sweetheart Wins Over the Wrong Michigan Suitor." *GenTales Magazine (online),* March 2020.

Molony, Janelle. "When the Earps Fought Indians," *Wild West Magazine*," (Forthcoming).

Molony, Richard. Oral History Interview by Joyce Hansen. *San Bernardino Oral History Project*. San Bernardino Public Library, January 14, 2003.

Muckenfuss, Mark. "Tales from the trail." *Press Enterprise,* August 2, 2014. https://www.pressenterprise.com/2014/08/02/muckenfuss-tales-from-the-trail/

Nollen, Carl. "Rousseau." *Marion County Genealogical Society Newsletter,* October (2020).

The 1864 Diary of Mrs. Sarah Jane Rousseau

Acknowledgements

A special thanks goes to named individuals who emphasized the value of this work and encouraged the continuation of study and preservation:

Val Val Kooten of the Pella Iowa Historical Society, Nicholas Cataldo of the San Bernardino Historical Society, Pamela Greenwood of the Curtis family, Stephen Daglish of the Daglish family (Sarah Rousseau's maiden name), Carl Nollen of the Marion County Genealogical Society, Rebecca Dockum for her research assistance, the many librarians and archivists at Central College of Pella, and especially to Richard Molony (Sarah Rousseau's 2nd great-grandson) for introducing me to the Rousseau story in the first place.

Without your support, this story, and the important discoveries within, might have been long lost to the world.

Janelle Molony

The 1864 Diary of Mrs. Sarah Jane Rousseau

A Sneak Peak...

In gratitude to the buyer, please enjoy an exclusive preview of the forthcoming fiction by award-winning author Janelle Molony, **From Where I Sat,** based on Mrs. Sarah Jane Rousseau's exquisite diary.

From Where I Sat (Excerpt):

Friday, March 11th, 1864
Knoxville, Iowa

Pulling back on the leather reins, the grayed and thickly bearded man halted his horse and cart in front of the Marion County Court House. He sat for a moment to let the dust settle around him while townsfolk passed by in their carts, carriages and on foot. Cottonwood trees peppered the city streets around the two-story white-washed building. The copper capped bell tower loomed over his horse and cart. He was grateful for the shade it lent.

Nicholas Earp reached up to his coat's breast pocket and pulled out a folded up, sweat-stained newspaper. He set down his copy of this week's *Burlington Hawk-Eye* on the cart bench, above where his canvas haversack lay slumped on the floorboard. On the page it was folded to, he could see the latest military announcements. One read:

"...There is talk about another call for men. As of yet, Government bounties are still being liberally paid. Those who have any thought to

enrolling in the army ought to do so at once, or else expect to be drafted without a dime."

Nicholas stepped down from the cart with a sigh. In a quick motion, he brushed both hands down the front of his dark blue wool coat and adjusted his medallioned hat.

"Last stop, Bud. I won't be long." Nicholas reached out a hand and patted his light brown, one-eyed horse before making his way up the brick steps to the courthouse's double doors. Wanted posters decorated a wood panel mounted near the entrance. The grim portraits exposed to sunlight were fading away, but the yellowing pages still promised a better payout than Nicholas ever received as a Provost Marshal. "Dead or Alive," one read. Now, draft evaders faced the same criminal punishment as the robber who'd blasted a hole through the center of the banker's vest.

"Uh-huh," Nicholas grunted as he scanned the faces, before running his tongue over his upper teeth to help him suction any scum off. Last August, he was nominated for sheriff of Marion County, but declined the venerable position. He was too old for chasing people anymore. He opened the doors to the incandescent-lit foyer and paused to adjust his eyesight from traveling in the bright sun.

"Hmm." The grand hall of the courthouse was empty. On either side were various county offices and smaller halls between them. Two broad staircases flanked the entrance. If Nicholas arrived after the offices closed, he'd have to wait until Monday to see about his inquiry. He heard a door open from down a hall ahead and paused to listen to the emerging voices.

John Hamilton walked towards the front exit of the building alongside the lawyer he worked as a clerk for. They had just debriefed from their afternoon trial on a small claims case.

"Well, I appreciate ev'rything you done, John. We won over the judge easily with that presentation." William Jesse Curtis shouldered his leather attaché. His golden brocade waistcoat and fawn colored tie complemented his brown jacket and hair perfectly.

The new lawyering job was turning out well for his friend, John reflected. As of last year, they'd been working together as law clerks for the Curtis family's firm until Jesse's father took a job at the county. While Jesse was studying for his bar exams, John helped him with his law school assignments. John admired Jesse's recent accomplishments, including joining the city council. Knowing John was part of those successes made him feel useful and appreciated.

"Heh, well, it's nothin'. I'm glad to help and I know your pa's real proud." John felt downright skinny next to his Herculean, yellow-blonde companion as they walked side-by-side down the hall. On the way, a coughing spell seized John. The rasp was as painful as it sounded. He grabbed a handkerchief from his pocket to cover his mouth.

Setting a hand on John's shoulder, Jesse offered, "Geeze, Johnny, it sounds worse than ever. You're going to get yourself checked, right?"

As the coughs subsided, John nodded and extended his right hand for a parting handshake. "I'm going right now. Promise. Just as soon as I get the ruling filed 'way."

"Great. I'll see you next week, then." Jesse nodded his parting as he passed by a fully uniformed man standing in the foyer as he left.

John noticed the man's striped shoulder patches, lowered his stack of papers and shoved his handkerchief into a pocket of his black trousers before standing tall, shoulders back. He cleared his throat and looked just past the man's piercing blue eyes. "Good afternoon, Sergeant."

"Mm-Hmm." Nicholas nodded with a polite grin. He was a third Sergeant, twenty years ago in the war with Mexico. Now, he spent most of his days tracking down Union rascals and Copperheads who wouldn't be patriotic to save their lives. Three years into this war and too many men had been slaughtered. The country had become increasingly more dependent on newly mustered youngin's who thought they could simply pick up a rifle and take aim without consequence. They were boys with new ideas. Boys without fathers to turn them into sensible men first. And Nicholas was supposed to be recruiting even more of them for the ongoing war effort.

He managed well enough doing so, until one of his sons came home a cripple. Not much good for anything now. Not on his left side, at least. The boy didn't even have a proper beard when he enlisted at nineteen.

This puny saluting man with a clean-shaven face looked to be his son's age. Nicholas twitched his mustache as he observed. Bloodshot eyes. His son James had them, too. "Are you Johnny, then?"

"Private Johnathan Bentley Hamilton, Sir. How can I help you?"

Nicholas removed his Union cap and held it down by his side. Immediately, the slim assistant's posture relaxed. Nicholas watched him press a palm over his greasy hair only to do not much more than flatten it.

"Is a lawyer in?"

"Sir, one just left."

"Yeah, I know." Nicholas regarded the young man who had already walked past him and out the doors. "Who else can I talk to about selling my property and settlin' my debts?"

"Well, no one's here excep' the government folk, Sir. It's almost closing time."

"I see that. So. Who's here?" Depending on who was around, perhaps Nicholas could use his military position to leverage his urgent request.

"The D.A. Try upstairs. Number three."

"That's good. Thanks." Nicholas patted John's shoulder and moved on to get himself an audience with the district attorney.

"Sir, it's Johnathan," the clerk asserted weakly. "You're welcome."

Nicholas ignored the man's anxious chatter and started up the west staircase. The legislative offices and courtroom were on the second level, as well as the judge's private study and chambers. The echoing, tiled building amplified the swish of Nicholas' thick pant legs, and the ca-lump of his brogan boots. It was more conspicuous than he preferred.

Door number three almost brought a laugh to Nicholas. The embossed door sign read Honorable Israel Curtis. "That's perfect."

As he hoped, Nicholas would have leverage here, but he also had a prior history to consider. If something went wrong, he'd lean heavily on his reformed reputation and, if needed, one small detail he'd come across this winter. With both hands, Nicholas smoothed his own thinning hair back before knocking.

The door opened to a brown suited gentleman with light hazel eyes and dirty blonde waves combed over neatly to the side. The D.A's thick brows rose in recognition of his old client.

Nicholas tapped the door sign with his hat and nodded an approval. "You're up top, now."

"Mr. Earp, yes. It's been a while. Are you starting trouble or stopping it these days?" Israel Curtis offered his right hand for a firm shake, then waved his guest in toward the mahogany desk. The office was downright spacious. And warm. A small coal stove sat to the right, near a pair of upholstered chairs, a small table, and a cabinet half of books. The forest green ingrain carpet made the room feel even more official. On the wall above Israel's desk, hung a miniature flag with thirteen stars and thirteen stripes.

Nicholas pressed his mustache down with his forefinger and thumb. "Just whippin' some folks into action," he summed.

The district attorney paused by his padded, black leather chair. He cocked his chin and remarked, "I hope not."

"Only those who deserve it," Nicholas clarified. He stood in front of the other chair, waiting to be seated. "You look presidential in here."

"I'm not sure I'd go that far, Mr. Earp. Have a seat."

Israel Curtis followed the movement of his visitor, leaning back slightly to catch a glimpse under the lip of his desk near where a revolver rested in a leather sling. "Just in case," his son Jesse had told him while loading the bullets. Israel never thought he would have a reason to even think of using the gun, but as the new district attorney, some folks might feel like holding him personally responsible for the discomfort they experienced due to the ruling on their case. He had to draw a line when Jesse suggested he carry a gun on himself while he preached the Sunday sermons. "The good Lord never needed a weapon to get his point across," he'd told his son.

"So, for what I do I owe the pleasure, Mr. Earp?"

Nicholas sat down and crossed his right ankle over his other knee then flicked two fingers toward the papers in Israel's painted tin trash bin. "Did you see the Burlington paper?"

"Burlington? No. Is that where you've been?"

"Yeah. Business." He tipped his head to the side and asked, "Do you know, folks in your field are giving amnesty to turncoat piles of sh—"

"Shh." Israel held up a hand to caution his old client. "Remember, I am a man of the church." Israel was one the lawyers who had found ways to soften the blow for Confederates who could show a good reformation. He sniffed, then continued.

"Forgiveness of sins is a Godly stance. But, from this pulpit, I would say that complete loyalty to one's leader is a noble and not oft'-found virtue. To imprison someone... or worse... for something that's not a crime if the same loyalty was offered to the Union would be hypocritical, wouldn't you say?"

Well, there went his military connection. Israel was a genuine Solomon. His mild manner and intensely green eyes made listening to his logic almost hypnotic. He deserved the "honorable" in his title.

"You make a good case." Nicholas needed to try harder to curry favor, not start a row. "I've been real loyal to the Union and protectin' its interests for a while. Serving my time. But..." He'd have to play just the right card. No one knew he'd put in to retire yet. "I'm thinkin' now's the time for me to get out of all this chaos that Governor Stone and others are stirrin' up 'round here. He's, uh, pushin' real hard for hittin' the enrollment quotas and repeat names are startin' to show up in the draft rolls..." It wasn't exactly the truth, but soon enough, it could be.

Looking up at Israel, he saw the man swallow and look away. Nicholas softened his voice a bit, then continued. "How many times do you think you can afford to pay your way out of seein' your son maimed and hardened by battle? A life for a lifetime of wages, when we could all jus' leave it be?"

Because of his position as the recruiter, Nicholas knew the Curtis family had paid for a draft exemption. Three hundred dollars with no guarantee the name wouldn't come up next round. He thought about the high-dollar rewards he saw posted in exchange for the life of a criminal. Some evil-doers are worth more than draft-evaders, but they keep their value when dead. It seemed a funny system to him.

Israel straightened up in his chair. "I've done what I could to keep 'em off the battlefield. Fair and square."

So far, he'd pulled every string he could to get his boys married and into critical careers. They weren't cut out for fighting. Israel's sons had higher callings on their lives. William Jesse, his eldest at twenty-six, just finished law school and had taken over the family law firm, Curtis and Curtis. Richard Henry, at twenty-one, didn't have the same level of aspirations, but had a good head about him. He might make a fine preacher one day. Clergymen were to be spared from the draft. But Richard had adamantly refused to participate in the church's affairs—not even for appearances.

"What are you getting at, Mr. Earp? And why are you coming to me?"

"I'm planning a trip to California. Out of the way. There's good soil, good weather, no trouble," he explained. "Now, what I need from you is to figure how I can start my residency there soon as possible."

"Stop beatin' around the bush, Earp."

"Alright." Nicholas slowed his speech. "I'd like my family to no longer be considered Iowans, even though I still need some time to sell off my property and get a wagon packed."

Israel furrowed his brows. "Are you sayin' you'd like me to fib on a property sale record and get myself mixed up in one of your schemes?"

Many years back, when the Earps first came to town, Nicholas hired Israel to reduce some criminal charges from an unpaid promissory note on an Illinois home. Israel also settled the claimant's attacks on the defendant for a bootlegging side operation—one that might even still be in business, Israel thought.

"Mr. Earp, I could charge you with a crime right now."

"Oh, with God as your witness?"

The two men locked eyes. Nicholas squinted. "I'm not askin' for anything illegal, I.C. I know exactly what this could cost me. So. I'm comin' to you for proper advice. Is there a way to get me and the boys off the roster, legally? I just need a head start."

Israel scoffed. He couldn't blame Nicholas for wanting the same thing he wanted, but crafting a cover-up was too risky in his position. As of February's new statutes, falsifying statements in favor of or causing an exemption were punishable to the same degree of a deserter. Still, in a way, Israel felt jealous of this man. Nicholas didn't have the means to pay an exemption fee for his sons, but he had courage to do something more drastic. As an unmarried man, Israel's son, Richard, was due to come up on the rolls again and again.

"I suppose I understand your position. But, I'm sorry, I'm not the person who can help you with this." Israel crossed his arms, hoping to settle himself.

Rising up, Nicholas paced a few steps, then said, "Listen, I got it all routed out. Three-to-four months of travel's all it takes. Then, we'll be so close to the sea, we can go pearl diving on Sundays." He stopped and corrected himself. "Or Saturdays."

Curiosity got the better of him and Israel asked, "What about the travel season, Earp? Folks are leaving right now to Oregon and Idaho. You won't have time enough to prepare for this stunt."

"Better late than never. I'm done with the Army and I'm done with Iowa, I.C. This is it for me and my boys."

By Israel's prior logic, being disloyal to the country wouldn't constitute a crime in God's eyes, if it meant being loyal to one's family. Sometimes this job meant using Godly wisdom instead of a mere human's ideas. Even the Israelites abandoned the wicked Pharaoh to follow God's plan of protection for their families. He nodded in response to his own internal justification.

"What's all that?" Nicholas pointed at Israel's head.

"I was wondering... If you know the way, would you consider taking another along?"

A spark lit in Nicholas' eyes. "Anyone? You thinkin' of smugglin' a stow'way in my wagon?"

With a sudden pound of his fist, Israel shouted, "Dang! No." Even Israel jumped at his own loss of composure. He looked up just past Nicholas to a filigreed oval frame featuring a stylish-looking woman in the center who'd faint over his reaction. She was expecting him for dinner.

"No. My son. Just—my son."

Nicholas turned and looked over his shoulder. "Ah. The blonde lawyer." He looked more closely at the family in the daguerreotype. "He takes after your wife."

Israel grew more irritated by the minute. This guy had turned the tables on him. "No. Not him." He stood up and came around the desk to face Nicholas. "But I think he can help you with your request, if you truly can help me with mine."

"I.C. If you can do this, I'll smuggle your whole damn family."

Israel put out his hand to shake on it. "To California."

Nicholas echoed, "To California."

Stay tuned for more information on this highly anticipated novel, coming to you soon!

Web: JanelleMolony.com/FromWhereISat
Social Media: Facebook.com/RousseauProject

About the Author & Editor

Janelle Molony is a family historian and nonfiction writer with prolific stories about individuals from the Civil War Era, Depression Era, and in Westward travel. Her work has been featured in the *Annals of Wyoming, Michigan Historical Review, Minnesota Genealogist, History Nebraska, Wild West* magazine, and many other notable publications.

Molony has won numerous awards from Writer's Digest, Readers' Favorite, BookFest, National Indie Excellence Awards, the National Federation of Press Women, and the Arizona Authors Association (and more).

In addition to writing, Molony has served as the oral history committee chair for the Wyoming Historical Society and is the program host their YouTube video series, "Women of Wyoming: Then & Now." She endeavors to continue freelancing, as long as her sweet husband is willing to put up with it. **Official: www.JanelleMolony.com**

Janelle Molony's Family Lineage

James Alexander Rousseau (1813-1882)

Sarah Jane Daglish (1815-1872)

1. Mary Ann Rousseau (1843-1882)
2. Sarah Elizabeth Rousseau (1849-1931)

    (md.) Walter Percival Cave (1843-1898)

    a. William Lee Cave (1869-1919)

    b. Florence Evelyn Cave (1871-1947)

    c. Sarah "Jenny" Cave (1874-1935)

    (md.) Joseph Auther Molony (1871-1940)

       i. Joseph Arthur Molony Jr. (1909-1970)

       ii. Walter Beverly Molony (1898-1974)

          (md.) Marguerite Elenor Robertson (1904-1948)

          1. Beverly Richard Molony (1926-2015)

          2. Ronald Molony (1933-2011)

3. Reginald Delbert Molony (1936-2019)
    a. Ryan Molony
    (md.) **Janelle Molony**

   d. James John Cave (1876-1905)
   e. Walter Percival Cave (1881-1905)
   f. Daisy Mae Cave (1884-1948)
   g. Lester Percival Cave (1887-1918)

3. John James Rousseau (1852-1914)
4. Albert Miller Rousseau (1856-1920)

Don't miss out on these other great reads from the historian you love!

From Where I Sat

(fiction, forthcoming) Web JanelleMolony.com/Rousseau Social Media @RousseauProject

Escaping the Civil War is extra hard when one's family is tied up in political schemes. To avoid the next round of drafts, a grand plan brings four families from Pella, Iowa together for the greatest adventure of their lives on the Overland-California trail. Between the endless starry nights and daytime gunfights with menacing Indians, Mrs. Sarah Rousseau logs the wagon train's progress in her pocket diary.

As a wheelchair-bound woman, she's not able to help when supplies run low and desperate choices must be made before they reach the snow-covered Sierra Nevadas standing between them and their California dreams. All she can do is write down what happens next. Follow all four families as they travel across the Plains together, for better or for worse.

"The balance of the journey, will be welcomed by trail fans."

Robert Clark, Overland-California Trails Association, Editor of *Overland Journal* (2020)

Emigrant Tales of the Platte River Raids

(non-fiction, 2023) Web JanelleMolony.com/EmigrantTales

While the Civil War raged in the east, the Platte River Raids would begin an entirely new battle for the American West. In July of 1864, Northern Plains Indians in Idaho Territory (Wyoming) appeared to be on a warpath to cease all emigrant travel on the Bozeman, Oregon, and Overland Trails by any means.

On a signal, hundreds of warriors launched a series of attacks and robberies on unsuspecting emigrants through the winding "Black Hills." Shots rang out and arrows whizzed as miners, doctors, farmers, families, and war widows rallied their covered wagons together. Some fought to defend their stock and protect their families. Others helped bury the bodies of those who did not survive.

Read the eyewitness testimonies of over 60 survivors, vetted by living descendants, mapped out, annotated, and presented in one accord for the first time in literary history.

"It's like having a front row seat for the action!"

Julia Brunia Thompsen, Descendant of the Jongewaard-Rysdam wagon train from Pella, IA (2023)

Now on sale!

Poems from the Asylum (non-fiction)

Web <u>JanelleMolony.com/PoemsFromTheAsylum</u>

Social Media <u>@SevenYearsInsane</u>

Biography and complete anth-ology of poems written in 1932 by Martha Nasch, patient-inmate #20864 at the St. Peter State Hospital for the Insane.

After noticing something strange from a secret medical procedure in 1927, St. Paul, Minnesota, Martha Nasch's doctor claimed she just had a "case of nerves." With a signature from her adulterous husband, Martha was committed against her will to the asylum. She spent nearly seven years in the Minnesota hospital during the Great Depression and tried to escape twice. Martha's poems from behind bars include shocking eyewitness accounts of patient treatment and a long-suffering adoration for her only child.

Inside, she sought an explanation for her mysterious condition that led her to a spiritual answer for the mystifying "curse." Would her findings make her a metaphysical guru of the Breatharian lifestyle, or would she become the laughingstock of her Depression-era family?

"Martha's story restores dignity and self-respect … to so many women diagnosed with a mental illness."

Mary Ann Lancette Palumbo, St. Paul Historian, MN (2022)

www.ingramcontent.com/pod-product-compliance
Lightning Source LLC
Chambersburg PA
CBHW080322080526
44585CB00021B/2433